PIXIE TO PROFIT

How to Build a Six Figure Business Offering One Haircut

Miko Pierson

CONTENTS

WELCOME!

Welcome to Pixie to Profit. I'm thrilled you're here, ready to discover what focusing on one specialty can do for your career, your business, and your life?

For years, I did what so many stylists do: I tried to offer everything, thinking it was the way to stay competitive. But I learned something powerful. It's not about doing it all—it's about doing one thing with such precision, skill, and passion that you become the go-to person. For me, that was the pixie cut.

When I dedicated myself to mastering the pixie, everything changed. My income stabilized, my brand grew stronger, and I found the kind of fulfillment that can only come from truly owning your craft. Through Pixie to Profit, I'm here to share how you can take this same approach and create a six-figure business built on your terms.

WHY THIS BOOK EXISTS

I wrote Pixie to Profit because I believe in the power of focus and mastery. This book isn't just about cutting hair; it's a guide to creating a business around your expertise, attracting clients who value your work, and building financial independence through doing what you love, and doing it exceptionally well.

In these pages, you'll learn:

- How to build the mindset and routines of a successful specialist.

- The pixie-cutting techniques that will set you apart and keep clients loyal.

- Strategies to brand yourself authentically, making it clear to clients why you're the best at what you do.

- Systems to create consistent, reliable income and make sure clients keep coming back.

- Ways to position yourself as a leader in your niche—because being great at one thing is how you stand out.

Each chapter offers insights you can put to work immediately. This book combines practical techniques with business-building strategies, so you'll have everything you need to turn your passion for this craft into lasting profit. And as you go through each chapter, remember to engage fully—take notes, practice the techniques, and apply what you learn.

This is Your Invitation to Focus and Thrive

If you've ever felt stretched too thin by offering every service, or if you've been looking for a way to simplify without sacrificing income, Pixie to Profit is here to show you a different path. This is an invitation to focus, to master, and to build a business around one thing that you do better than anyone else.

I'm sharing everything I've learned so you can find the same freedom and stability that specialization has given me. Pixie to Profit is built on the belief that you don't need to do it all to make a great living— you just need to master what you love and make it your own.

Thank you for choosing this journey with me. I can't wait to see how you make Pixie to Profit your own story of success.

Preview: What You'll Discover in Pixie to Profit

Imagine This

Picture yourself as a stylist whose clients don't just visit once—they return again and again, specifically for your expertise. You've become known for something unique, something you've mastered down to the finest detail. For you, that specialty is the pixie cut, and it's more than just a haircut; it's the foundation of a six-figure career.

In Pixie to Profit, you'll see how focusing on one style can transform your business and your life. This book will take you through each step, from mastering the technical skills to branding yourself as a go-to expert, all the way to building a business that brings both profit and purpose.

What's Inside

Throughout this book, you'll explore the steps that lead to mastery and the strategies that build a business around it. Here's a quick look at what each chapter will bring:

Chapter One: Building the Foundation – Mindset, Mastery, and Confidence – Success starts with the right mindset, strong physical presentation, and daily routines. This chapter sets the foundation for long-term growth and mastery in your craft.

Chapter Two: Becoming a Pixie Pro – Mastering the Cut – Mastering the pixie cut requires precision and technique. This chapter breaks down every detail you need to create flawless, customized cuts.

Chapter Three: Creating the Signature Pixie Experience – Clients return for more than just a haircut—they come for the experience. Learn how to craft each appointment into a personalized, memorable session that builds loyalty.

Chapter Four: Elevating Your Reputation Through Presence and Expertise – Your brand is your identity in the industry. This chapter guides you in establishing a strong presence that naturally attracts your ideal clients.

Chapter Five: Building Lasting Client Relationships and Loyalty The key to a thriving business is retaining happy, committed clients. Discover strategies to build trust, deepen relationships, and create lasting client loyalty.

Chapter Six: Systems for Stability—Creating Consistent Wealth through Reliable Processes – Financial stability comes from well-structured systems. Learn how to streamline processes that support consistent income and long-term success.

Chapter Seven: The Growth Mindset—Investing in Your Continued Development – Growth doesn't stop once you master the basics. This chapter teaches you how to evolve, invest in yourself, and continuously elevate your skills.

Chapter Eight: Navigating Challenges—Turning Obstacles into Opportunities – Challenges are inevitable, but they don't have to be setbacks. Learn how to adapt, pivot, and turn difficulties into stepping stones for success.

Chapter Nine: Beyond the Chair—Building a Career that Impacts and Inspires – Your influence extends beyond the salon chair. This chapter explores ways to expand your career through education, leadership, and brand-building.

Chapter Ten: Living Financial Freedom—Breaking Free from the Need for Variety and Focusing on Wealth – Success isn't about doing everything—it's about doing one thing exceptionally well. Learn how to create wealth and freedom by focusing on your expertise.

A Path to Real Success

Pixie to Profit is about more than just cutting hair—it's about turning your craft into a lasting career with real financial impact. If you're ready to focus, master, and create a six-figure business doing what you do best, this book is for you. Each chapter is crafted to give you actionable insights and step-by-step strategies to help you build your brand, create consistent income, and make an unforgettable impact on your clients.

Get ready to start this journey. By the end, you won't just be offering a haircut; you'll be delivering an experience, a brand, and a reputation that keeps clients coming back.

FOREWORD

I entered corporate America shortly after college and had my first child soon thereafter. Navigating life as a businesswoman in the fast-paced Metropolitan Washington, D.C., while juggling motherhood and longing for even a sliver of a social life, was no easy feat. I quickly learned to "outsource" some of my recurring tasks to masters of their craft in an effort to reclaim some of my time. Washing, conditioning, blow-drying, and roller-setting—affectionately called "doing hair"—became the number one task I realized I needed to offload to a professional.

The D.C. Metropolitan area, also known as the "Mecca" for upwardly mobile Black people in the U.S., was where you could find the brightest, most cutting-edge professionals, including top-notch hair stylists. During the decade I called the DMV home, I was fortunate to have a bi-weekly standing appointment with Shirley, an award-winning, celebrity hair stylist who, over the years, became so much more than my stylist. She became a confidant, a teacher, a friend, a source of wisdom, and the epitome of a businesswoman. And every single time, she perfected my hair.

When an opportunity arose for me to relocate to North Carolina, I cried about leaving two pillars of my life: my church home and my hairstylist. I thought they were irreplaceable. I vowed to my D.C. stylist that I would not leave her until she could refer me to someone "just like her." After nearly a year of commuting from North Carolina to D.C. bi-monthly for hair appointments, my stylist finally shared a name she had heard buzz about in the industry: Tamiko, based in Durham, NC.

My first appointment with Tamiko was in 2007. She seamlessly treated and styled my hair with the same perfection I was accustomed to, and I have been a faithful client ever since. Over the past seventeen years, we have cultivated a solid friendship. Year after year, I have watched Tamiko constantly strive to elevate her craft. In the past two decades, she has become a salon owner, a national educator for one of the top global haircare systems, an industry influencer, an author, a brand creator, and one of the most sought-after stylists in North Carolina. There isn't anything the powerhouse known simply as "Miko" cannot conquer with poise, professionalism, and sheer expertise.

A few years ago, Miko pivoted to become a Pixie Powerhouse—slaying the pixie cut to perfection while maintaining her passion for teaching others in her industry. It has been an honor to be a passenger on Miko's extraordinary journey. She embodies Martin Luther King Jr.'s quote, "You don't have to see the whole staircase, just take the first step."

Through her mastery of the pixie cut, Miko not only transformed her career but created a roadmap for others to follow. This book will empower you to do the same, unlocking the secrets to earning six figures with one haircut while making a lasting impact in your clients' lives.

Readers, you are in for an amazing treat filled with authenticity and expertise—buckle up!

Ife Mitchell-Parks

Sr. Enterprise Account Executive

Chapter One: Building the Foundation – Mindset, Mastery, and Confidence

One of my early coworkers, Tim, had this incredible way of presenting himself—he wasn't just there to "do a job." Most days, he'd come in dressed up, excited, and ready, and it wasn't just in his clothes. It was his energy, his words, and the way he interacted. When clients asked, "Why are you dressed up today?" he'd simply say, "My look reflects how I feel about my work."

But Tim's preparation went beyond appearance; he knew how to tune into each client. Sometimes, he'd bring high-pitched excitement, creating a lively, uplifting experience. Other times, he'd adopt a calm, studious tone, describing his process with focus. Watching him match his clients' moods and consistently bring passion to his work left a lasting impression on me. It challenged me to ask myself: How can I keep elevating what I offer?

I realized that if I wanted to earn my clients' trust and loyalty, I needed to show up fully—both in my presentation and in the energy I brought to my work. Tim's example inspired me to focus on lifelong learning, on routines that prepared me to surprise my clients, and to show up every day with the same intention he did. That approach— grounded in mindset, presentation, and routines—has become my foundation for success.

Introduction to the Foundation of Success

Building a Six-Figure Career Starts Here

When you think about reaching six figures with a single haircut, it's not just about skill—it's about having the right foundation. Everything starts with your mindset, how you present yourself, and the habits you commit to daily. It's the work you do behind the scenes that sets you up for success, far beyond what happens with a client in your chair.

Becoming a specialist isn't for everyone, but if you're serious about mastering the pixie cut and turning it into a profitable career, it's time to get focused. This isn't about offering a dozen services, chasing trends, or trying to please everyone who walks through the door. This is about becoming known for what you do best and building a reputation that keeps clients coming back.

In this chapter, we're going to set the foundation. I'm going to show you how to shift your mindset from generalist to specialist, how to develop the confidence that clients trust, and how to establish routines that keep you on track. You'll learn how small changes in the way you think and the way you carry yourself can make a big impact—not only on your career but on the way clients see you and value your work.

Why Your Mindset Matters

Before you pick up a pair of shears, your mindset has already shaped how you show up. To build a six-figure career offering one haircut, you need a mindset that's focused, resilient, and ready to commit to mastery. This means moving past the idea that you need to offer variety to be valuable. Instead, we'll focus on becoming known for what you do better than anyone else.

So let's start building the foundation. If you're ready to focus, commit, and set yourself up for true success, then let's dive into what it takes to make that happen.

The Power of Mindset for a Specialist

Think Like a Specialist, Not a Generalist

In this industry, it's easy to get caught up in the idea that success means being able to do everything. But when you try to offer it all, you end up spreading yourself thin—and clients notice. To reach six figures, you need to shift from a generalist mindset to a specialist's mindset. Instead of trying to please everyone, focus on what you do best and dive deep into it. Mastering the pixie cut is about more than just knowing how to execute the style; it's about becoming so good at it that people seek you out specifically for it.

A specialist doesn't just follow trends—they set them. They know their worth and don't feel pressured to offer everything under the sun. This mindset shift allows you to stand out, create demand, and ultimately, build a brand around your expertise.

What Success Looks Like When You Focus

Imagine being the go-to stylist for pixie cuts in your area. Clients walk in knowing you're the best at what you do, and they leave thrilled with results they can't get anywhere else. They aren't choosing you based on price—they're choosing you based on expertise. When you're known for a specific skill, you don't have to compete with other stylists on variety or even availability; clients will make time to book with you.

So take a moment to define what success looks like for you in this context. Maybe it's consistent income that lets you work smarter, not harder. Maybe it's building a client base that respects your time and talent. By focusing on one area, you set yourself up for the kind of success that comes from being the best at what you do, rather than just one of many.

Practical Mindset Shifts for a Six-Figure Career

Here are three mindset shifts that will help you build the foundation for success as a pixie specialist:

1.   Quality Over Quantity: Instead of trying to fill your schedule with as many clients as possible, focus on quality. Deliver a service that exceeds expectations every time. When clients feel that

you're giving them your full attention and expertise, they're willing to pay more—and keep coming back.

2.   Value Your Expertise: Stop viewing your skill as "just a haircut." The pixie cut is your craft, your brand, and your business. When you treat it with that level of respect, your clients will too. They'll see the value in what you offer and understand that it's worth paying for.

3.   Commit to Lifelong Learning: Being a specialist doesn't mean you stop learning once you've "made it." True mastery comes from continuous improvement. Make a commitment to keep honing your skills, trying new techniques, and deepening your understanding of the pixie cut.

Exercise: Define Your Specialist Mindset

Take a few minutes to answer these questions:

1.   What does being a "pixie specialist" mean to you? How would you describe this role to a client?

2.   What does success look like in this niche? (Think beyond money—consider lifestyle, client relationships, and reputation.)

3.   How will you continue to learn and grow in this specialty? What steps can you take to keep your skills sharp and evolving?

Write your answers down and revisit them as you move forward in this book. These answers will serve as your personal guide and help you stay focused on your goals.

Why Your Mindset Sets You Apart

Clients can tell when a stylist is confident and committed to their craft. When you approach your work with the mindset of a specialist, clients feel it. They know they're not just getting a haircut—they're getting a level of care, detail, and expertise that only comes from true mastery. This mindset becomes part of your brand. It's what clients remember, it's why they recommend you, and it's what keeps them coming back.

Building Confidence through Consistency

Confidence is Built on Repetition and Routine

Confidence doesn't just show up overnight. It's built through repetition, through doing the work and refining your skills day after day. When you focus on one thing, like mastering the pixie cut, you're giving yourself the chance to build confidence in a way that would be impossible if you were constantly jumping from style to style. With each client, your hands get steadier, your eye gets sharper, and your results get stronger.

Consistency isn't just about skill development—it's also about the experience you provide to your clients. When clients know they can expect the same high level of service every time they walk into your chair, it builds trust. That trust is invaluable. It's what makes clients loyal, what brings them back, and what gets them talking about you to their friends. The more consistent you are, the more confidence you'll have, and the more confidence clients will have in you.

Why Consistency Sets You Apart

Think about the last time you went to a new restaurant. If the food and service were great, you might go back. But if your second experience didn't measure up, you'd probably hesitate to recommend it to friends. The same is true in the beauty industry. Clients need to know that every time they book with you, they're getting the same high-quality experience.

When you become known as a pixie specialist, your reputation is tied to your ability to deliver consistent results. It's not enough to have one great day in the salon; it's about showing up fully for every client, every appointment. Consistency is what separates a true specialist from just another stylist.

The Confidence-Consistency Connection

Consistency isn't just about your skill with the shears—it's about how you carry yourself, how you communicate with clients, and how you follow up. Confidence comes from knowing that you can provide the same level of excellence, time and again, and that clients can rely on you. The more you focus on consistency, the stronger your confidence will grow, and the more it will show in your work.

Here's how to build consistency into every part of your service:

1.   In Your Technique: Refine your techniques until they're second nature. Practice the same steps in your cuts, and approach each new client with a similar routine. Consistency in technique means fewer mistakes, smoother processes, and better results.

2.   In Your Communication: Clients appreciate clarity and honesty. Be clear about what you're doing, what to expect, and how to maintain their style at home. Consistency in your communication builds trust and makes clients feel valued.

3.   In Your Personal Standards: Hold yourself to high standards every day, not just on days when you feel energized. The way you present yourself, your punctuality, and your attention to detail all contribute to the experience you provide. Consistency in these areas shows clients that you're committed to excellence.

Exercise: Developing Your Consistency Checklist

To make sure you're delivering a consistent experience every time, create a checklist of standards you commit to for each client. This could include:

- Greeting each client warmly and with a smile.
- Taking time to listen to their needs before starting.
- Following a set routine for each cut, from sectioning to finishing.

- Checking in with the client throughout the appointment to ensure satisfaction.
- Giving clear instructions for at-home maintenance.

Once you've created your checklist, keep it somewhere visible, like your station or your phone. This will remind you to bring your best to each appointment, no matter how busy or tired you are.

The Power of Routine in Building Your Confidence

Confidence isn't just about what you can do—it's about how you feel while doing it. When you have a routine, you're not scrambling to figure things out as you go. You're focused, calm, and fully present. Routines help reduce anxiety and eliminate guesswork, allowing you to focus entirely on your client and the experience you're creating. When clients feel that focus, they feel valued and respected, and that creates loyalty.

Your routine could include everything from how you prepare your station before a client arrives to how you wrap up the appointment. By following a routine, you're training yourself to work at a higher level, and that sense of calm confidence will become second nature over time.

-

Physical Presentation – Looking the Part

Your Image Reflects Your Expertise

When clients sit in your chair, they're trusting you to make them look and feel their best. But that trust doesn't just come from your skill with a pair of shears; it's also influenced by how you present yourself. In this industry, image matters, and if you want clients to see you as a specialist, you need to look the part.

Your physical presentation—everything from your attire to your hygiene to your energy—sends a message before you even say a word. Are you dressed in a way that shows you take your craft seriously? Does your style reflect the kind of work you do? These details matter more than you might think. Clients pick up on everything, and they'll feel more confident in your skills if you look like someone who's committed to quality and professionalism.

Why Presentation Impacts Client Trust

Clients come to you because they want to feel confident and stylish, and they'll look to you for inspiration. Think about it: if you're branding yourself as the go-to pixie specialist, clients will naturally expect your style to reflect your expertise. This doesn't mean you need to look a certain way, but it does mean that every detail—your hair, attire, even your workspace—should show that you care about quality and presentation.

Looking the part goes beyond aesthetics; it's about setting a standard. When clients see that you hold yourself to high standards, they'll feel reassured that you'll apply that same care and precision to them. Your look tells clients that you respect your craft, and that respect will earn their trust.

Elements of a Polished Presentation

Looking the part doesn't mean you have to dress up or put on a show. It's about intentional choices that align with the brand and reputation you're building. Here's what to focus on:

Personal Grooming: Clients will notice if you're well-groomed. Take time to make sure your hair, nails, and hygiene reflect the standards you hold for your work. Your attention to these details shows that you respect yourself, which sets the tone for how others respect you.

Professional Attire: Dressing professionally doesn't mean wearing a suit or uncomfortable clothes. Instead, wear something that makes you feel confident, capable, and ready to work. Choose attire that fits your style but also feels polished. Think of your outfit as part of the client experience—it's another way you're showing clients what you stand for.

Posture and Body Language: How you carry yourself says a lot about your confidence and professionalism. Stand tall, make eye contact, and engage with clients in a way that shows you're fully present. Clients want to feel seen and valued, and your body language can reinforce that connection.

A Welcoming Workspace: Your station or suite is an extension of your brand. Keep it clean, organized, and stocked with the tools you need. When clients see a tidy, well-maintained space, it gives them a sense of confidence that you're organized, reliable, and prepared.

Exercise: Assess Your Presentation

Take a moment to evaluate your physical presentation with these questions:

1.   If a client walked in right now, would your look reflect your standards?

2.   Does your style align with the brand you're building as a pixie specialist?

3.   Is your workspace clean, organized, and welcoming?

4.   Do you feel confident and capable in your appearance?

If there's room for improvement, set one or two small goals to elevate your presentation. These could be as simple as updating your wardrobe to reflect your brand more closely or setting a routine to tidy your workspace between clients.

Creating a Lasting Impression

Physical presentation is one of those subtle things that has a huge impact on how clients perceive you. When you look and act the part of a specialist, clients will feel they're in good hands. And when clients trust you, they're more likely to come back, refer friends, and invest in your services.

Your image is part of your brand. It's one of the first things clients notice and one of the last things they remember. Make it count. By holding yourself to high standards in your physical presentation, you're reinforcing the message that you're a professional with a passion for quality. This kind of impression can't be faked—it has to be earned, and it's worth every effort.

Daily Routines that Support Mastery

Success is Built in the Day-to-Day

When you're working toward mastery, every day matters. It's not just about showing up for clients—it's about showing up for yourself. Building daily routines that support your goals keeps you grounded, focused, and always moving forward. A strong routine eliminates the guesswork and helps you show up prepared and ready, no matter how busy things get.

The routines you set now will help you develop the consistency, confidence, and resilience you need to become a true specialist. These habits might seem small on their own, but they add up, creating a solid foundation for success.

The Importance of Routine for a Specialist

When you're striving to be the best at one thing, like the pixie cut, your focus is intense. You're working with precision and detail, honing skills that clients expect you to have mastered. Routines keep you sharp and efficient, so that when you're with a client, you're fully present and able to give them your best.

By building habits around preparation, reflection, and even self-care, you're creating a system that helps you thrive. It's not just about doing the work; it's about doing it with purpose and consistency.

Key Routines to Support Your Growth

Here are some powerful routines that can help you stay focused on your path to becoming a six-figure specialist:

1. Pre-Client Preparation: Take a few minutes before each client to mentally and physically prepare. Review any notes you have on them, set up your tools, and take a breath to clear your mind. When you start each appointment focused and prepared, clients notice. They'll feel like they're your top priority because, in that moment, they are.

2. Post-Client Reflection: After each client, take a moment to assess the experience. Did the cut go as planned? Did the client seem satisfied? Was there anything you'd change next time? By reflecting after each appointment, you're constantly learning and adjusting, which strengthens your skills over time.

3. Skill-Building Time: Set aside time each week just for skill-building. Whether it's practicing a new technique, watching tutorials, or revisiting the basics, dedicating time to improve your

craft keeps you competitive and sharp. Even a half-hour of focused practice can make a big difference over time.

4.   End-of-Day Review: At the end of each day, take a few minutes to review how things went. This can include checking your appointments for the next day, tidying up your workspace, and jotting down any notes on client preferences or techniques to try. This review clears your mind and prepares you for the next day, so you're not carrying work stress home with you.

5.   Self-Care and Recharging: Consistency and confidence require energy, so make self-care part of your routine. Eating well, exercising, and getting enough rest aren't just nice to have—they're essential. When you take care of yourself, you're able to bring your best self to each client and maintain a high level of performance.

Exercise: Create Your Daily Success Routine

Take a few minutes to outline your ideal daily routine. Here's a template to get you started:

- Morning Prep: What will you do each morning to get ready for the day?
- Pre-Client Ritual: How will you prepare for each client to ensure you're focused and ready?
- Skill-Building Practice: How often will you dedicate time to practice and refine your skills?
- End-of-Day Review: What can you do at the end of each day

to close out your work and prepare for tomorrow?

- Self-Care: What routines will help you recharge and stay balanced?

Once you've written out your routine, keep it somewhere you can see it daily. Over time, these habits will become second nature, creating a foundation of consistency and confidence that your clients will feel in every appointment.

Why Routines Lead to Results

When you're working to become the best at what you do, your daily routines become your structure and your support. They help you show up consistently, stay focused on your goals, and make gradual improvements that add up over time. This commitment to routine is what sets a specialist apart from the crowd. It's the behind-the-scenes work that fuels your success and keeps clients coming back for the consistent, high-quality experience they trust.

Mastery isn't about big leaps—it's about the steady, daily commitment to getting better. When you invest in your routines, you're investing in yourself and your career. So, take the time to create routines that support your growth and keep you moving forward. Your clients will notice, and your career will reflect it.

Mindset Exercises for Long-Term Growth

Keeping Your Mindset Strong and Focused

Mastery isn't a destination—it's a journey of constant improvement. And while daily routines and technical skills are essential, a growth-oriented mindset is what keeps you moving forward. When you're committed to a niche, like the pixie cut, your focus needs to be sharp, resilient, and adaptable. These mindset exercises are designed to help you stay connected to your goals, stay motivated, and keep growing in the long run.

Exercise 1: Setting Intentional Goals

Goal-setting isn't just about achieving milestones; it's about staying motivated and giving yourself a clear direction. To get the most out of this exercise, think beyond just numbers or financial targets. Consider what kind of impact you want to make and how you want your career to feel.

- Instructions: Write down three goals for your career as a pixie specialist. Make them specific, measurable, and meaningful. For example:
- "I will become the go-to pixie specialist in my city by increasing client referrals by 20% this year."
- "I will dedicate 30 minutes a week to skill-building to improve my techniques and stay ahead."
- "I will improve client retention by focusing on

creating a memorable experience for each client."

Review these goals regularly, and adjust them as needed. Let them serve as a reminder of the bigger picture you're working toward.

Exercise 2: Visualizing Success

Visualization is a powerful tool for building confidence and maintaining focus. When you visualize yourself succeeding, you're mentally rehearsing the outcomes you want to create, which helps strengthen your belief in your abilities.

•   Instructions: Each morning, take a few minutes to visualize a successful day. Picture yourself confidently performing a perfect pixie cut, interacting with happy clients, and feeling energized and focused. Imagine clients appreciating your expertise, referring friends, and returning for your specialized services. This simple practice helps set a positive tone for the day and keeps your mind focused on success.

Exercise 3: The Gratitude Shift

Staying grateful for your progress and small wins keeps you motivated, even when challenges arise. It shifts your focus from what's lacking to what's growing, reinforcing a positive mindset that supports long-term success.

•   Instructions: At the end of each day, write down three

things you're grateful for in your career. They can be small wins (a client complimenting your work) or long-term achievements (a new referral, positive feedback, etc.). Over time, this habit helps you stay focused on the progress you're making, keeping your mindset positive and forward-focused.

Exercise 4: Monthly Self-Assessment

Growth requires honest reflection. Every month, take time to assess your progress, celebrate wins, and identify areas for improvement. This isn't about criticizing yourself; it's about keeping an honest eye on your development.

- Instructions: Set aside 15-20 minutes at the end of each month to review your goals, routines, and overall growth. Ask yourself:
  - "What went well this month? What am I proud of?"
  - "Where did I face challenges, and what can I learn from them?"
  - "What's one thing I can improve or adjust next month?"

This self-assessment keeps you grounded in your journey and helps you make small, meaningful adjustments to stay on track.

Building a Growth Mindset

These exercises are simple but powerful tools to keep your mindset strong and growth-focused. By setting goals, visualizing success, practicing gratitude, and assessing your progress, you're reinforcing the belief that every day brings an opportunity to improve. Mastery doesn't happen by accident—it's the result of a consistent commitment to growth, one step at a time.

So, make these exercises a part of your routine. They'll help you stay motivated, keep your focus sharp, and remind you that every effort you put in brings you closer to the success you envision.

Wrap-Up and Next Steps

The Foundation of Your Success

In this chapter, you've laid the groundwork for a successful career as a pixie specialist. You've seen how the right mindset, consistent routines, and a commitment to growth set you apart from the crowd. Becoming a six-figure stylist starts here—with a solid foundation built on focus, confidence, and resilience.

Remember, this path isn't about doing everything; it's about mastering one thing and doing it exceptionally well. Each day, as you refine your skills, improve your routines, and strengthen your mindset, you're taking steps toward becoming the go-to expert your clients can rely on.

Next Steps

Now that you've set the foundation, it's time to dive deeper into your craft. In the next chapter, we'll focus on the techniques, tools, and strategies that will help you master the pixie cut. You'll learn the details of shaping, refining, and perfecting this iconic style, turning it into an experience that clients won't find anywhere else.

So, take a moment to revisit the exercises, keep your goals in mind, and prepare to go even deeper into the art of the pixie cut. This is where your journey toward true expertise begins.

Chapter Two: Becoming a Pixie Pro – Mastering the Cut

When I first started in this industry, fresh out of beauty college, I thought I was ready. I was confident in my waving, marceling, and other skills I'd worked hard to develop. But haircutting? That was a different story. I learned just how much work I had to do when I sent some clients to a fellow stylist while I was on vacation. She sent word back, saying, "Thanks for the referrals, but don't send your clients to me for my cutting skills. You gotta learn that on your own!"

That was my wake-up call. It was embarrassing, yes, but it also lit a fire in me. I knew I had gaps to fill, and I was ready to get serious about mastering the cut. From that moment on, I invested time, energy, and effort into learning everything I could. I dove deep into technique, understanding the shapes, angles, and textures that make a pixie cut work. Precision became my focus, and I practiced until every cut was consistently sharp and tailored. I developed an eye for detail, knowing that each line, each angle, played a part in bringing the client's vision to life. Communication became key; I practiced listening and talking with clients to ensure I fully understood their ideal look. By asking the right questions, I could make sure we were aligned before I ever picked up the scissors. Over time, I built the skill and confidence to deliver that same high-quality cut every time, creating trust and consistency that formed the foundation of my reputation.

Introduction to the Pixie Cut

Why the Pixie Cut is Iconic

The pixie cut is more than just a hairstyle—it's a statement. It's bold, stylish, and versatile, and it never truly goes out of fashion. For decades, the pixie has been a favorite of those who want a look that's both classic and edgy. It's flattering, low-maintenance, and adaptable to countless variations, making it one of the most timeless cuts in the industry.

But the pixie is also a cut that requires precision, creativity, and an eye for detail. Unlike longer styles, a pixie cut leaves little room for error. Every angle, every texture, every line is on display. This is why clients will seek out a true specialist—someone who knows how to make the pixie look effortless yet polished, chic yet personalized.

The Art of Specializing in the Pixie

When you specialize in the pixie cut, you're setting yourself apart in a way that clients notice. This isn't just a quick, one-size-fits-all style; it's a cut that demands skill and intuition. You'll need to understand how to create balance, how to shape a cut to suit each client's features, and how to add those subtle details that make a pixie stand out.

Clients will come to you because they trust you to give them a look that complements their face shape, hair texture, and lifestyle. They're looking for a stylist who knows the ins and outs of this cut and who can deliver it with confidence and precision. In this chapter, we're going to break down the techniques, tools, and skills that will help you master the art of the pixie cut.

The Basics of Pixie Shaping

Shaping the Foundation of the Pixie Cut

When it comes to the pixie cut, shaping is everything. Unlike longer styles, where you can rely on layers or length to create movement, the pixie is all about precision. Every angle and section matters, and the way you shape the cut from the very beginning sets the tone for the final look.

Shaping a pixie cut is about building a foundation that complements each client's unique features. It requires attention to detail, a steady hand, and a clear vision of the final shape. By understanding the basics of pixie shaping, you'll be able to create a structured, balanced cut that brings out the best in your clients.

Core Techniques for Sectioning and Balance

The pixie cut is typically divided into key sections that allow for better control and balance. Here's a simple approach to sectioning that will keep the cut clean, organized, and aligned with the client's head shape:

1.   Fringe (Bang) Area: This is one of the most defining parts of a pixie cut and can drastically alter the final look. The fringe can be blunt, side-swept, or texturized, depending on the style you're creating. Begin by sectioning off the fringe to allow for more control later in the cut.

2.   Top Section: The top section determines the cut's volume and shape. This is where you'll decide on the length, texture, and how it flows into the rest of the cut. For a fuller look, leave more weight here; for a sleeker look, keep it shorter and closer to the scalp.

3.   Crown Area: This is the section where you can add subtle lift and shape. The crown area should blend seamlessly with the top and back of the head, creating a smooth transition that complements the client's natural head shape.

4.   Sides and Back: The sides and back provide structure and frame the face. When cutting these areas, pay close attention to the angle and length to ensure they flow naturally into the rest of the style. This is where precision is crucial, as even the smallest difference in angle can alter the overall look of the pixie.

5.   Nape: The nape area gives the pixie its clean, tailored finish. This section often requires tapering or texturizing to create a polished look that aligns with the client's head shape. A shorter nape

offers a bold, defined look, while a slightly longer nape can soften the style.

Balancing the Cut with Face Shape

Every face is unique, and a well-shaped pixie cut will bring out the best in a client's features. Here's a guide to balancing the pixie with different face shapes:

- Round Faces: For round faces, aim to add height at the crown and avoid too much volume at the sides. A slightly longer fringe can help create a more elongated look, giving the face a balanced shape.
- Square Faces: Square faces benefit from softer edges and texturized layers that add movement. Avoid blunt cuts around the jawline, as these can accentuate the squareness of the face. A side-swept fringe can soften the look and add a touch of asymmetry.
- Oval Faces: Oval faces are the most versatile and can pull off nearly any pixie style. Play with volume, texture, and fringe length to enhance the client's natural symmetry.
- Heart-Shaped Faces: For heart-shaped faces, keep the cut balanced by adding volume around the jawline and avoiding too much height at the crown. A soft, layered fringe can help soften the forehead and bring balance to the overall look.
- Long Faces: For long faces, aim for more width in the cut. Volume at the sides and a full fringe can help balance the length of the face, giving it a more proportionate appearance.

Using Angles and Elevation for Shape Control

In a pixie cut, the angles and elevation you use while cutting directly impact the final shape. Here are some essential techniques to keep in mind:

1.   45-Degree Elevation: This angle is great for adding volume and lift, especially at the crown. When you elevate the hair at 45 degrees, you're creating a natural, rounded shape that gives the pixie its soft, feminine edge.

2.   90-Degree Elevation: This angle is ideal for creating even layers throughout the cut, providing a balanced and structured look. A 90-degree elevation is commonly used on the top and sides to maintain length while removing bulk.

3.   Low Elevation (0–15 Degrees): For the nape and areas where you want a close, tapered effect, keep the elevation low. This creates a clean, defined finish that's polished and professional.

Precision and Attention to Detail

The pixie cut is unforgiving when it comes to mistakes. Unlike longer styles, where minor errors can be hidden in layers, every detail of a pixie cut is on display. This is why precision is key. Work slowly, check your angles frequently, and step back to assess the overall shape as you go. Consistency in your technique is what sets apart an average pixie from an exceptional one.

Refining Techniques for Texture and Dimension

Adding Life to the Pixie with Texture and Dimension

One of the key features that clients love about a great pixie cut is its versatility and movement. When done right, a pixie can look soft, edgy, sleek, or voluminous—all with a few strategic techniques. Texture and dimension are what make a pixie unique to each client, allowing you to tailor the style to suit their personality and preferences.

In this section, we'll look at the texturizing techniques and layering methods that bring out the best in a pixie cut. By learning to create depth and dimension, you'll transform each cut from basic to beautiful, ensuring that no pixie you create looks flat or lifeless.

Point Cutting for Softness and Movement

Point cutting is one of the most effective ways to add subtle texture to a pixie cut. This technique involves cutting into the ends of the hair at an angle, creating a softer, more natural look. Here's how and when to use point cutting in a pixie:

1. Softening the Fringe: Use point cutting to break up a blunt fringe and give it a softer appearance. This technique works especially well for clients who want a more relaxed, casual style.
2. Adding Movement to the Crown: Point cutting at the crown adds movement, creating lift and preventing the top from

looking too heavy. It allows the hair to move more freely, adding dimension without extra bulk.

     3.   Texturizing the Sides: Point cutting along the sides of the pixie can help blend the layers seamlessly into the rest of the cut, creating a cohesive look. This is especially helpful for clients with thick hair who want a sleeker style.

When using point cutting, be mindful of the depth of each cut. A light touch will give a subtle texture, while a deeper angle will create a more dramatic, piecey effect. Tailor the depth to the client's preference, whether they want soft texture or bolder separation.

Texturizing Techniques for Volume and Dimension

Texturizing techniques go beyond basic cutting and add character to the pixie. Here are a few essential texturizing techniques that can give your pixie cuts the added volume and dimension clients crave:

     1.   Slide Cutting: Slide cutting involves gently gliding the shears down the length of the hair, removing weight while keeping the length. This technique is ideal for creating a soft, blended look that has natural movement. Use slide cutting on the top and sides for a more dynamic, less structured style.

     2.   Channel Cutting: Channel cutting is a method where you create small channels or grooves within the hair to reduce bulk and add separation. By working vertically through sections of the pixie, you can create volume and depth that give the cut a modern, edgy vibe. Channel cutting works well on clients with thick hair who

want a lighter, more texturized finish.

3.   Razor Texturizing: Using a razor can give the pixie cut a slightly undone, feathered effect. Razors remove weight while keeping the edges soft, making them ideal for clients who want a relaxed, bohemian look. Be cautious when using a razor—too much pressure can thin the hair too much, especially on finer textures.

4.   Thinning Shears: Thinning shears are perfect for removing bulk without changing the overall shape of the cut. These shears can add lift at the crown or soften a heavy fringe. Use them sparingly on finer hair to avoid creating unwanted gaps or a choppy appearance.

Layering Techniques for Depth and Shape

Layering is essential in a pixie cut, as it creates the framework that gives the style its structure and movement. Here's how to use layering to your advantage:

1.   Internal Layers for Volume: By adding internal layers, you can create volume from within the cut without sacrificing length. Internal layers are great for clients with thicker hair who want a pixie that looks full but not bulky.

2.   Graduated Layers for Softness: Graduated layers are shorter at the bottom and gradually lengthen toward the top, creating a soft, cascading effect. These layers work well for clients who want a pixie that hugs the nape while giving fullness around the crown.

3.   Disconnected Layers for Edge: Disconnected layers add a modern, edgy twist to the pixie cut. By keeping some sections

slightly longer or shorter than others, you create a unique, personalized look. Disconnected layers work best for clients who want something bold and aren't afraid to experiment with texture.

4. Stacked Layers for Definition: Stacked layers are typically shorter in the back and build length toward the front. They add definition and structure, giving the pixie a clean, defined shape. Stacked layers are ideal for clients who want a classic, polished pixie with a bit of volume.

Blending for a Natural Finish

A well-executed pixie cut should look seamless and natural, with no visible "steps" or hard lines between sections. Blending is the final step to ensure the cut flows smoothly and suits the client's features. Here's how to approach blending:

• Use a Comb to Check Transitions: As you move through each section, use a comb to check for smooth transitions between layers. Any visible lines or uneven sections can be blended with point cutting or thinning shears.

• Adjust for Hair Texture: Blending techniques vary based on hair texture. For thicker hair, use deeper texturizing techniques to reduce bulk. For finer hair, keep blending subtle to maintain fullness and avoid creating gaps.

• Step Back and Assess the Overall Shape: After blending each section, take a step back and view the entire cut. Look for areas that may need extra blending, and ensure the cut has a cohesive, balanced shape.

Adding Depth and Character

A great pixie cut has depth and character that make it unique to the client. By combining these texturizing and layering techniques, you can give each pixie a personalized look that sets it apart. Your goal is to create a cut that not only suits the client's features but also enhances their natural texture and brings out their personality.

These techniques are what transform a basic pixie into something truly exceptional. With practice and a bit of creativity, you'll be able to customize each cut to achieve the perfect balance of texture, volume, and dimension—ensuring that no two pixies you create are ever the same.

Customizing the Pixie for Each Client

Making the Pixie Cut Personal

No two clients are alike, and the pixie cut should reflect that. When someone sits in your chair, they're looking for more than just a stylish cut—they want something that's made for them. This is where you take your pixie skills to the next level by tailoring the cut to fit each client's face shape, hair type, and personal vibe.

A one-size-fits-all approach doesn't work here. Your job is to make adjustments that enhance their best features and bring out their personality. A truly customized pixie cut has a level of confidence and sophistication that clients can feel. Here's how to make each cut a signature look that's all their own.

Understanding the Client's Vision

Before you even pick up your shears, start with a clear, open conversation. The pixie cut is a bold choice, and clients often have a specific vision in mind—even if they can't quite articulate it. Ask questions to understand what they're looking for, and guide them toward options that will work best for their features.

- Ask Targeted Questions: What do they love about the pixie? Are they looking for something soft and feminine, or bold and edgy? Do they want something low-maintenance, or are they open to styling at home? Questions like these give you insight into their preferences and lifestyle.
- Listen and Guide: Sometimes clients come in with a specific idea based on a picture they've seen. Your job is to interpret that idea while being realistic about what will actually work for them. This is where your expertise comes in—show them options that suit their unique look, and explain how you'll customize the cut to make it their own.

Tailoring the Pixie to Face Shape

One of the most important aspects of customizing a pixie cut is tailoring it to the client's face shape. A well-suited cut can highlight their best features and bring balance to their look. Here's how to adjust for different face shapes:

- Round Face: To elongate a round face, create height at the crown and keep the sides closer to the head. A slightly longer fringe that sweeps to one side can also add length, giving the face a more balanced look.

- Square Face: For a square face, soften the angles by adding texture around the edges. Avoid blunt lines near the jawline, and consider a side-swept fringe that adds movement and softens the overall look.

- Oval Face: An oval face is versatile and can handle most pixie styles. Play with the fringe and volume to create a balanced cut. For an edgy twist, you could even experiment with disconnected layers or bold texturizing.

- Heart-Shaped Face: Balance out a heart-shaped face by adding volume around the jawline. Avoid too much height at the crown, which could make the forehead appear wider. A layered fringe that softens the forehead can bring balance to this shape.

- Long Face: To balance a longer face, create width with a fuller fringe or added volume at the sides. Avoid too much height, as this can elongate the face further. Layering around the sides can create the illusion of more width.

Each face shape has its own needs, so adjust accordingly. When you get this right, clients will feel the difference—and they'll keep coming back because they know you "get" them.

Adjusting for Hair Texture

Texture plays a huge role in how a pixie cut looks and feels. Not every client has the same hair type, and knowing how to work with different textures will help you create a cut that's easy for them to maintain and style.

- Fine Hair: Fine hair can look flat if it's too short, so add internal layers to create volume without sacrificing length. A soft fringe and a bit of height at the crown can help make fine hair look fuller.
- Thick Hair: Thick hair requires weight removal to avoid a bulky look. Use slide cutting, point cutting, or thinning shears to take out excess weight. A razor can also be helpful to create a softer, feathered effect that keeps the cut light and airy.
- Curly Hair: For curly hair, keep the length a bit longer to allow the curls to show their natural shape. Avoid over-layering, as this can cause frizz. Work with the natural curl pattern and add subtle texturizing only where needed.
- Coarse Hair: Coarse hair often benefits from a bit of tapering to reduce bulk. Use thinning shears to blend and soften the cut without removing too much weight. A polished nape and structured top can create a sleek, defined look.

When you tailor the cut to suit their texture, clients will notice how much easier it is to style and manage. They'll appreciate the difference it makes to have a pixie that's designed with their hair type in mind.

Bringing Their Style to Life

Finally, make the cut reflect who they are. A pixie cut is a strong style choice, and the finishing touches can make it feel edgy, soft, classic, or trendy, depending on the client's personality.

- Soft and Feminine: For clients who want a gentle, feminine look, go for softer edges and subtle texturizing. A soft fringe and smooth lines can make the pixie look relaxed and approachable.
- Edgy and Bold: If your client wants something bold, experiment with disconnected layers, asymmetrical fringe, or a tapered nape. Don't be afraid to use razors or clippers to add a unique edge.
- Classic and Polished: For a more classic look, keep the cut structured and avoid excessive texturizing. A neat nape and clean lines create a timeless, polished effect.
- Modern and Trendy: For clients looking to stay on trend, play with length and fringe options. A long fringe with a shorter back or adding a pop of color can give a modern twist that keeps the cut current.

Each client is looking for something that feels right for them, so pay attention to their personality and preferences. A pixie cut that matches their style will make them feel authentic and confident—and that's what keeps clients loyal.

Advanced Pixie Finishing and Detailing

The Finishing Touches That Make the Difference

A well-executed pixie cut isn't just about the shape and texture—it's about those finishing details that bring the entire look together. The finishing stage is where you elevate a basic cut into a statement piece, adding the precision and polish that clients expect from a specialist. These details may seem minor, but they make a huge impact on the final look and feel of the style.

In this section, we'll go over techniques that ensure every pixie you cut has a smooth, seamless finish. From using the right tools to refining the lines, these steps add the kind of polish that leaves clients feeling like they're wearing a custom piece.

Using Tools for Precision and Polish

The right tools allow you to create a clean, polished finish that highlights your attention to detail. Here's how to use razors, clippers, and shears for those finishing touches:

1.   Razor for Soft Edges: A razor can give the pixie cut a softer, feathered edge, especially around the fringe or nape. This tool is ideal for clients who want an "undone" look without sharp, blunt lines. Lightly use the razor to create a feathered effect on areas that need a softer finish.

2.   Clippers for Clean Lines: Clippers can create a

precise, structured finish, especially at the nape and sides. For a more polished look, use clippers to clean up the nape and give the cut a crisp edge. Adjust the length settings to control how close you want the cut to the scalp.

3. Point Cutting Shears for Texture: Point cutting shears are perfect for adding subtle texture and movement to the ends. Use them sparingly on sections that need a bit of extra lift or definition, such as the fringe or crown. This technique prevents the cut from feeling too "solid" and adds a sense of lightness.

Detailing the Nape for a Polished Finish

The nape area is a focal point in a pixie cut, and getting this part right is essential for a professional finish. Clients will notice if the nape is uneven, too bulky, or poorly blended, so take your time here. Here are some techniques to perfect the nape area:

• Tapering for a Tailored Look: Use clippers or shears to taper the nape, creating a clean line that fits closely to the neck. This adds structure and gives the cut a polished look that grows out gracefully. Tapering also prevents the cut from looking too heavy at the base.

• Blending for a Seamless Transition: Blending is key to ensuring the nape flows naturally into the rest of the cut. Use thinning shears or point cutting to blend the nape into the sides and crown, creating a smooth, seamless look. Check your work from multiple angles to make sure there are no harsh lines.

• Detailing with Clippers: For clients who want an

edgy, defined nape, use clippers to create sharp lines or an undercut. This can add an unexpected twist to a classic pixie, giving it a more modern, fashion-forward edge.

Refining the Fringe for Balance and Style

The fringe (or bangs) is another defining feature of a pixie cut. It frames the face and can be styled in multiple ways to suit the client's preferences. Here's how to refine the fringe for balance and impact:

- Side-Swept Fringe for Softness: A side-swept fringe is flattering on most face shapes and adds a touch of softness. Use point cutting to break up the ends slightly, ensuring the fringe flows naturally into the rest of the cut.
- Blunt Fringe for Boldness: For clients who want a bold look, a blunt fringe can create a strong statement. Keep the line sharp and even, and avoid over-texturizing to maintain the impact of the blunt cut. This style works best on clients with straight or fine hair.
- Textured Fringe for Movement: A textured fringe adds a relaxed, effortless vibe. Use point cutting or a razor to create separation and movement in the fringe, making it feel lighter and more dynamic. This style works well for clients with wavy or curly hair.

Final Check and Client Experience

Once you've completed the finishing touches, take a moment to step back and assess the cut from all angles. This final check ensures everything flows smoothly and aligns with the client's vision. It's also a great time to ask the client for feedback and make any last-minute adjustments.

• Check for Symmetry: Look at the cut from all sides to ensure symmetry, especially around the fringe and nape. A balanced cut is essential for a professional finish.

• Adjust Based on Client Feedback: Ask the client how they feel about the cut and be open to making small tweaks. This level of care shows that you're invested in their satisfaction and willing to go the extra mile to deliver a look they love.

• Teach At-Home Styling Tips: Show clients how to style their new cut at home, recommending products and techniques that suit their hair type. This helps clients feel confident maintaining their look, and they'll appreciate the added value you provide.

Delivering a Finished Look that Lasts

Finishing and detailing aren't just about looks—they're about creating a cut that grows out well and stays stylish in between appointments. These final touches set the pixie apart, leaving clients with a style that feels polished and personal. With the right finishing techniques, you're giving clients more than a haircut; you're giving them a look that's built to last.

Exercise: Perfecting Your Pixie Practice

Putting Theory into Practice

Mastering the pixie cut takes more than just reading techniques—it requires hands-on practice, repetition, and a commitment to refining your skills. This exercise section is designed to help you turn what you've learned into consistent, high-quality results. These exercises will push you to focus on precision, texture, and balance, ensuring each pixie you create meets your high standards.

Set aside time each week to work on these exercises, and remember: every small improvement adds up to make a big difference. Whether you're practicing on a mannequin or a willing client, these drills will build your confidence and elevate your pixie game.

Exercise 1: Sectioning and Shaping Drill

Purpose: To build precision and control in the foundational structure of the pixie cut.

- Instructions: Begin by sectioning the hair into the key areas: fringe, top, crown, sides, and nape. Focus on creating clean, even parts and clearly defining each section. Once sectioned, practice shaping each area with the basic angles—45-degree and 90-degree elevations. Pay attention to your hand positioning and ensure each section flows naturally into the next.
- Goal: Develop muscle memory for clean sectioning

and consistent shaping, making it second nature in every cut.

Exercise 2: Point Cutting and Texturizing Practice

Purpose: To refine your skills in adding texture and dimension without over-thinning.

- Instructions: On a mannequin or model with medium-thickness hair, practice point cutting the fringe, crown, and sides to add subtle texture. Use a light touch to avoid removing too much weight, and focus on creating a balanced, natural look. For added challenge, use different depths of point cutting to explore how each variation affects the style.

- Goal: Gain confidence in texturizing with point cutting, so you can add movement and dimension without losing control of the cut's shape.

Exercise 3: Blending and Smoothing Transitions

Purpose: To ensure smooth transitions between sections for a cohesive, polished look.

- Instructions: Practice blending each section of the pixie, especially where the top meets the sides and the crown blends into the nape. Use thinning shears or slide cutting to smooth transitions, then comb through each area to check for evenness. Take time to view the cut from multiple angles to ensure consistency and balance.

- Goal: Master the art of blending, creating a cut that's seamless and visually appealing from every angle.

Exercise 4: Nape Detailing and Edge Work

Purpose: To enhance your precision with clippers and shears for a clean, defined nape.

- Instructions: Use clippers or a razor to practice detailing the nape area. Start with a longer guard, then gradually work your way to shorter lengths, tapering carefully for a tailored finish. Experiment with both sharp, defined lines and softer, feathered edges. Check for symmetry and adjust as needed to achieve a balanced look.
- Goal: Build precision and confidence in detailing the nape, ensuring a polished, professional finish every time.

Exercise 5: Personalizing the Pixie for Different Face Shapes

Purpose: To develop a natural instinct for tailoring the cut to each client's features.

- Instructions: On three different mannequin heads (or models with varying face shapes), practice adjusting the pixie to suit each face type. Focus on creating different fringe styles, adjusting volume placement, and tailoring the overall shape to complement each face. Assess the final look and make tweaks as needed.
- Goal: Strengthen your ability to analyze face shapes and adjust your approach, making each cut feel custom and

intentional.

Building Confidence Through Practice

Practice makes perfect, but purposeful practice builds mastery. These exercises are designed to help you break down the pixie cut into manageable skills, so you can master each part with confidence. Commit to practicing consistently, and over time, you'll notice your cuts becoming cleaner, more balanced, and uniquely tailored to each client. Every minute you put into perfecting these details is an investment in your skill and your reputation as a pixie specialist.

Wrap-Up and Next Steps

Mastering the Art of the Pixie

In this chapter, you've explored the techniques and skills that turn a pixie cut into a true work of art. From shaping and texturizing to refining the final details, you now have the tools to create a customized, polished cut that suits each client's unique style and features. A well-executed pixie cut isn't just about the basics—it's about the precision and personality you bring to every appointment.

Remember, mastering the pixie cut is a process, and each cut you create is an opportunity to refine your skills. With practice, these techniques will become second nature, allowing you to deliver consistently beautiful results that clients won't find anywhere else.

Next Steps

Now that you've built the foundation and mastered the technical skills, it's time to focus on the client experience. In the next chapter, we'll dive into the details of creating an experience that goes beyond the haircut itself. You'll learn how to make every client feel valued, understood, and excited to return—not just for the cut but for the connection they feel with you.

Get ready to elevate your client relationships to match the level of skill you bring to the chair. Together, these elements will create a powerful, memorable experience that keeps clients coming back and recommending you as the go-to pixie specialist.

CHAPTER THREE: CREATING THE SIGNATURE PIXIE EXPERIENCE

One of my clients, Ms. Mildred, was a cancer survivor with hair loss from her treatments. When we met, I had just shaved my hair, so there we were, sitting together in the hallway with our bald heads, talking before I even started her appointment.

We connected instantly, reminiscing about her childhood and her father's natural, clean lifestyle as a Rasta. I could see how much that way of living meant to her, and I reminded her how powerful it could be to reconnect with that lifestyle. When she handed me her wig to cut, I noticed the lingering smell of glue in it. Even though it wasn't going on her scalp, I couldn't ignore it. I said, "You know, our skin is the biggest organ—it absorbs everything. If it were me, I wouldn't want to wear this."

I offered to reach out to someone who could create an organic wig for her, one free from chemicals, and she lit up. That small gesture made her day. She didn't just find a new stylist; she found someone who shared her values and cared about her well-being. By the end of our conversation, she told me she's usually the type to "get in and get out," but that day was different. We'd created a bond—a sisterhood—by sharing openly and prioritizing what truly mattered to her. That experience showed me that when you bring your genuine self, share openly, and make your client's well-being a priority, you're not just offering a service—you're creating a memorable experience.

The Importance of the Client Experience

Why the Experience Matters as Much as the Cut

In the beauty industry, it's easy to focus solely on technical skill, but the truth is, the client experience is just as important. Clients come to you not only for your expertise with the pixie cut but also for the way you make them feel. A great cut is memorable, but a great experience is what builds loyalty, trust, and lasting relationships. The way clients feel in your chair—valued, understood, and appreciated—makes them eager to return and recommend you to others.

When you create a signature client experience, you're offering something that goes beyond the cut. You're building a relationship that keeps clients coming back, not just because of the result but because of the connection they feel with you. This connection is what separates a one-time appointment from a loyal client who trusts you with their look and refers friends to your chair.

The Power of a Signature Experience

The goal is to make every client feel like they're getting something unique, a cut and experience that can't be found anywhere else. A signature experience isn't about doing something flashy or over-the-top; it's about the small touches and personalized moments that show clients you care. This can be as simple as remembering their preferences, checking in throughout the appointment, or following up after a big style change.

A memorable client experience also helps protect your reputation as a specialist. When clients feel valued and understood, they're more likely to give constructive feedback, trust your recommendations, and refer you with confidence. The stronger the experience you provide, the more your brand grows through positive word of mouth.

Experience Over Price

Clients who feel a connection with their stylist are less likely to shop around based on price alone. When they value the experience you provide, they're willing to invest in your expertise, knowing they're getting more than just a haircut. This is why your client experience isn't just an add-on—it's a crucial part of your business strategy. It's what sets you apart and positions you as the go-to pixie specialist they can rely on.

Creating a Welcoming Atmosphere

Your Space Sets the Tone

Before a client even sits in your chair, they're already forming an impression of you. Your space—whether it's a private suite, a station, or an entire salon—tells clients a lot about your professionalism, style, and the experience they're about to have. A welcoming atmosphere doesn't just happen by accident; it's something you create intentionally, with every detail working to make clients feel comfortable, relaxed, and valued.

Creating a space that feels both inviting and professional is key. A clean, organized environment reflects your commitment to quality, while personal touches show that you care about your clients' experience. Your space should feel like an extension of your brand, setting a tone that makes clients feel like they're in good hands.

Setting Up an Inviting Space

An inviting space doesn't have to be elaborate, but it does need to feel intentional. Here are a few tips to make sure your space feels welcoming:

- Keep it Clean and Tidy: A clean space shows clients that you respect your work and value their time. Regularly sanitize your tools, sweep your station, and organize supplies between appointments. These small details don't go unnoticed—they reassure clients that you're attentive to their safety and comfort.
- Add Personal Touches: A few well-chosen decorations, like fresh flowers, a favorite piece of art, or a scented candle, can make your space feel personal and warm. These touches make clients feel like they're in a place that's thoughtfully designed, not just another chair.
- Comfortable Seating: Clients may spend some time

waiting, so make sure the seating area is comfortable and inviting. Offer a clean, well-cushioned chair, and consider providing small comforts like a magazine, water, or tea. These small gestures show that you care about their experience from the moment they walk in.

• Lighting and Music: Soft, natural lighting and gentle background music can do wonders for setting the mood. Bright, harsh lighting can feel uncomfortable, while softer lighting creates a warm, relaxing atmosphere. Music that matches your brand—calm and soothing or upbeat and trendy—can make clients feel like they're in an experience curated just for them.

Your Demeanor Creates Comfort

A welcoming atmosphere isn't just about the physical space; it's about the energy you bring into it. Your demeanor sets the emotional tone for the appointment, influencing how clients feel in your chair. A friendly, calm, and confident approach puts clients at ease and allows them to feel comfortable communicating their needs and preferences.

• Greet Clients Warmly: From the moment they walk in, make clients feel valued. Greet them by name, offer a warm smile, and make eye contact. This simple greeting establishes a connection and shows that you see them as more than just a client.

• Show Genuine Interest: Take a few minutes to ask how they're feeling, what they're looking forward to, or how their day is going. Clients want to feel like you care about them as individuals, not just as appointments. These small moments of connection build trust and make them feel appreciated.

• Stay Calm and Focused: Clients pick up on your energy, so approach each appointment with calm, focused attention. Even on busy days, take a deep breath before each new client to reset. This calm presence helps clients feel they're in capable hands, ready for a great experience.

Creating a Relaxed Vibe

A big part of making clients feel welcome is creating a relaxed atmosphere that helps them unwind. Clients often see a haircut as a form of self-care, so make it feel like a break from their everyday routine. Here are a few ways to make the experience feel more like a treat:

• Offer Refreshments: A glass of water, coffee, or tea can make clients feel more at home. It's a small gesture that says you care about their comfort and want them to feel at ease.

• Encourage Open Communication: Let clients know that they're welcome to share their thoughts and feedback at any time. Reassure them that you're here to help them achieve a look they love, and that their satisfaction is your priority.

• Be Attuned to Client Preferences: Some clients love to chat, while others prefer a quiet, relaxing experience. Pay attention to their cues and match your energy to their comfort level. If they seem like they want to talk, engage with genuine interest. If they're more reserved, allow them to relax without forcing conversation.

Why the Atmosphere Matters

A welcoming atmosphere isn't just a nice extra—it's a core part of the client experience. When clients feel comfortable and valued, they're more likely to open up about their style goals, trust your expertise, and walk away with a positive impression of your brand. An inviting space and a calm, friendly demeanor make clients feel they're getting more than just a haircut—they're getting a full experience that's all about them.

By creating a welcoming atmosphere, you're setting the stage for a memorable appointment. Clients will leave feeling like they've been taken care of, and they'll be excited to return to a place that feels like their own personal escape.

Mastering the Consultation

The Consultation is Key

The consultation is one of the most important parts of any appointment. It's your opportunity to understand what the client wants, assess what will work best for them, and build a shared vision for their look. When done well, a consultation not only clarifies expectations but also builds trust and sets the client at ease. They'll feel heard, respected, and excited for what's to come.

A great consultation isn't just about asking questions; it's about reading between the lines, understanding client needs, and guiding them toward the best version of their desired style. This is where you demonstrate your expertise and set the tone for a personalized experience they won't get anywhere else.

Ask Open-Ended Questions to Understand Their Style

Start with open-ended questions to get clients talking about what they want. The goal is to let them express their preferences, concerns, and hopes for the cut without feeling rushed or judged.

- Examples of Open-Ended Questions:
- "What do you like most about the pixie cut?"
- "How do you usually style your hair on a daily basis?"
- "Is there anything you'd like to change or improve about your current style?"

These questions encourage clients to share their vision and give you valuable insights into their lifestyle, maintenance preferences, and style goals. Let them talk, and take notes to remember specific details they mention.

Listen and Repeat Back for Clarity

Active listening is key to making clients feel heard and understood. As they share their thoughts, nod to show you're engaged, and repeat back key points to confirm you've understood. This doesn't just help with clarity—it also builds trust and makes clients feel valued.

- Example: If a client says they want a low-maintenance look, respond with, "So you'd prefer something easy to style and that doesn't need a lot of upkeep?" This confirmation shows that you're paying attention and helps prevent misunderstandings.

Listening also gives you a chance to notice any inconsistencies. If a client says they want something low-maintenance but mentions loving a very styled look, you can gently guide them toward a compromise that suits both needs.

Guide Clients Toward What Will Suit Them Best

As a specialist, clients rely on your expertise to help them make decisions. If a client's vision doesn't align with what will realistically work for them, it's your role to guide them to a style that suits their features, hair type, and lifestyle. Approach this part with a gentle, encouraging tone—they need to feel that you're on their side.

- Frame Suggestions as Collaborative Ideas: Instead of saying, "That won't work for you," try, "I have a few ideas that could work really well with your face shape. Let's look at some options together." This keeps the conversation positive and reinforces that you're working with them to find the best solution.
- Educate Without Overwhelming: Explain why certain cuts or textures might not work as well with their features, but keep it simple. For example, "A longer fringe could add a nice softness

70

around your face," or, "With your hair texture, a bit more length here will help the cut stay low-maintenance."

By guiding clients in this way, you're not just helping them make a choice—you're also building your reputation as a trusted expert who has their best interests at heart.

Showcase Visuals to Solidify the Vision

Visuals can be incredibly helpful in ensuring you and the client are on the same page. Have a few pictures or examples of different pixie styles ready, and use these to show clients how certain styles will look. Visuals help clients better understand what certain terms mean (like "soft layers" or "textured fringe") and make it easier for you to explain your ideas.

- How to Use Visuals in the Consultation:
- Show a range of styles to gauge their reactions. Watch their face as you present each image—this can tell you a lot about what they're drawn to.
- Use visuals to highlight small variations within the pixie cut, such as length at the nape, fringe options, or levels of texture.
- Encourage them to bring their own pictures or inspiration. Seeing what they're inspired by helps you understand their taste and expectations.

Set Realistic Expectations with Honesty and Positivity

Not every client request is realistic, and part of your role as a specialist is to manage expectations while keeping the client excited about their look. Be honest about what will work with their hair type and features, but keep the tone positive. Clients appreciate honesty, especially when it comes from a place of care and expertise.

- Example: If a client with fine hair requests a high-volume pixie style that won't be achievable, you could say, "Your hair texture is naturally finer, so achieving that exact volume daily might be challenging. But I can create a similar look with some added texture that will be easy to style and maintain."

Setting realistic expectations helps prevent disappointment and reinforces the client's trust in you. They'll leave knowing that you're invested in giving them a look that works for them, not just a trendy style that may not hold up in real life.

Create a Plan for At-Home Maintenance

Once you've established the cut, give clients a few simple tips on how to maintain their look at home. This shows that you're invested in helping them keep their style looking great beyond the appointment. Whether it's recommending specific products, styling tools, or techniques, these small tips add value to the experience.

- Examples of At-Home Tips:

- Show them how to use a styling cream to add texture or define layers.
- Explain how often they should get trims to keep the cut in shape.
- Suggest a quick, easy way to refresh their fringe in between appointments.

Clients appreciate these tips, and they'll leave feeling empowered to maintain their look. Plus, it adds to the personalized experience, making them feel like you've thought of every detail just for them.

Bringing It All Together

Mastering the consultation is about more than just asking questions—it's about creating a shared vision with the client, understanding their needs, and guiding them with expertise and care. When clients feel heard and involved, they trust you, relax, and get excited about the cut. A strong consultation sets the tone for the entire appointment, making the client feel like they're in the hands of a true professional who values their satisfaction.

Building Trust Through Consistency

Consistency Creates Confidence

One of the best ways to build a loyal client base is through consistency. When clients know they can rely on you to deliver the same high level of service and quality every time they come in, they don't just see you as a stylist—they see you as a trusted professional. Consistency isn't just about the final cut; it's about every part of the experience, from the initial greeting to the final styling tips.

Clients who can count on you will keep coming back, not just for the results but because they trust you with their look and know what to expect from each appointment. By showing up consistently, you're telling clients, "You're in good hands."

Start with a Consistent Greeting and Approach

Your consistency begins the moment clients walk in the door. Greet each client warmly, just like you did at their last appointment. This isn't about being robotic; it's about creating a dependable experience that makes clients feel valued and welcomed each time.

• Establish a Routine: From the greeting to the consultation, set a routine that you follow with each client. This could mean always starting with the same open-ended question about their hair goals, or taking a moment to recap their last appointment. A routine shows clients you're organized and attentive, and it sets a professional tone right from the start.

• Stay Present and Focused: Even if you're having a busy day, make sure each client feels like they have your full attention. Avoid distractions, and focus on their needs throughout the appointment. Consistency in your focus reassures clients that they're your priority, no matter what's happening around you.

Deliver Consistent Quality Every Time

Your technical skill is a huge part of what keeps clients coming back, so make it a goal to deliver the same quality every time. Clients expect their cut to look just as good on their third appointment as it did the first time they came in. Here's how to ensure you're meeting their expectations:

- Refine Your Techniques: Practice the techniques you use in every cut so they become second nature. Consistent quality isn't about doing things exactly the same way each time, but about ensuring that the results are consistently excellent. When you're confident in your methods, it shows in the cut and reassures clients that they're getting the best.

- Check Your Work Thoroughly: Before finishing, take a moment to step back and check the cut from all angles. Look for any uneven spots, blending issues, or areas that could use a bit of refinement. A quick double-check ensures that each cut meets your high standards, showing clients that you don't rush or cut corners.

- Stick to Your Style: Clients come to you because of your unique approach to the pixie cut. Maintain the signature style and techniques that make your work stand out. Consistency in your style is a key part of building your brand, making clients feel like they're getting a personalized look that's distinctly yours.

Consistency in Communication and Follow-Up

Clients value clear, reliable communication. Be consistent in how you communicate expectations, style tips, and follow-up recommendations. This consistency not only enhances their experience but also builds their confidence in your expertise.

- Offer Reliable Styling Tips: If you've shown them a particular technique for styling their cut, check in at the next appointment to see how it's going. Reassure them that you're there to support them beyond the chair. This follow-through makes clients feel that you're invested in their satisfaction, not just the immediate results.

- Set Realistic Maintenance Schedules: Be consistent in recommending a realistic schedule for trims and touch-ups. Explain how often they should come in to keep the cut looking fresh, and let them know why regular maintenance is essential for the pixie cut. This builds trust by showing that you care about their look long after they leave the salon.

- Create a Routine for Follow-Ups: For new clients or clients trying a big style change, consider a quick follow-up message or call to see how they're feeling about the cut. A simple check-in shows that you care about their satisfaction and are open to feedback.

Reliability Builds Relationships

Consistency might seem like a small thing, but it has a big impact on your reputation. When clients know they can rely on you, they feel confident not only in your skills but also in your dedication to them as individuals. This reliability builds relationships that go beyond a single appointment—clients see you as someone they can count on, whether it's for their next trim or a recommendation on products.

Your consistency becomes a part of your brand. It's what makes clients trust you, refer you, and keep coming back, knowing that they'll receive the same level of care and quality every time. In the end, consistency isn't just a practice; it's a promise to your clients, one that they'll remember long after they leave your chair.

Creating Moments of Connection

Small Gestures, Big Impact

A great haircut is important, but it's the little things that make clients feel truly valued. Creating small, meaningful moments during the appointment helps clients see that you care about them as individuals, not just as clients. These moments of connection don't have to be elaborate or time-consuming; they're simple gestures that make a big impact and show clients that you're invested in their experience.

Moments of connection are what turn an appointment into a memorable experience. They help clients feel relaxed, seen, and understood, fostering a sense of loyalty that keeps them coming back. Here's how to build those connections effortlessly.

Remember the Details

Taking note of personal details—whether it's their favorite way to style their pixie, a big event they're preparing for, or even something they shared last time about their family—shows clients that you remember and care. Mentioning these details during their next appointment goes a long way in creating a bond.

- Examples:
- "How did your hair work out for that wedding you mentioned last time?"
- "I remember you prefer your fringe a bit longer—are you still liking it that way?"
- "Did you enjoy that vacation you were planning? I'd love to hear about it!"

These small details make clients feel like you truly listen to them, not just as clients but as people. They're reminders that you're paying attention and that they're more than just a name on your schedule.

Offer a Genuine Compliment

Everyone likes to feel appreciated, and a sincere compliment can make clients feel great about themselves and their look. Whether it's about their hair, their sense of style, or their energy, a genuine compliment can brighten their day and make them feel at ease.

- Examples:
- "You always pull off this look so well—it really suits your style."
- "I can tell you take such good care of your hair; it's so healthy!"
- "You have such a positive energy—it's always a pleasure having you in my chair."

Compliments should feel natural, not forced. If you notice something you genuinely admire about a client, let them know. It's a simple gesture that leaves a lasting impression.

Check in During the Appointment

Throughout the appointment, take a moment to check in with your client about their comfort, satisfaction, and overall experience. These small check-ins make them feel that you're attentive and focused on their needs.

- Examples:
- "Are you comfortable? Let me know if you need anything."
- "How are you feeling about the cut so far?"
- "Is there anything you'd like me to adjust or change as we go?"

This kind of proactive care makes clients feel safe in your hands, knowing that their comfort and satisfaction are your top priorities.

Celebrate Their Style

When a client tries a new look or returns for a style they love, take a moment to celebrate their choice. Show enthusiasm and support for their decision, and let them know that you're excited about how the look reflects their personality.

- Examples:
- "This cut is so bold—it really matches your vibe."
- "I love how this style brings out your features—it's perfect for you."
- "It's always fun to try something new, and you pull it off beautifully!"

When clients feel that you're as excited about their look as they are, it reinforces their confidence in their choice and in your expertise.

Why Connection Matters

Moments of connection don't just enhance the appointment—they create a sense of loyalty and trust. Clients remember the way you make them feel, and these small gestures show them that they're more than just another client in your day. By creating genuine connections, you're building a reputation as a stylist who cares, listens, and values each client as an individual.

In the end, these connections are what turn clients into long-term supporters of your business. They leave the appointment not only with a great haircut but also with a sense of being appreciated and understood. And that's the kind of experience they'll be eager to come back to—and tell others about.

Exercise: Crafting Your Signature Client Experience

Turning Techniques into Your Unique Approach

Now that you've explored what makes a powerful client experience, it's time to make it your own. Every stylist brings something unique to the table, and this exercise is about identifying and defining those qualities that set you apart. Crafting a signature client experience isn't about doing everything perfectly; it's about creating a style that feels authentic to you and resonates with your clients.

When clients come back because they appreciate the way you make them feel, you've done more than just create a great haircut—you've built a brand. Use this exercise to put intention behind each step of the experience, so every client leaves knowing exactly why they chose you.

Step 1: Define Your Client Interaction Style

Think about the energy and tone you want to bring into each appointment. Are you laid-back and conversational, or more reserved and focused? Knowing your natural style will help you create an experience that feels genuine and effortless.

• Write Down Your Approach: Describe in a few words how you'd like clients to feel in your chair. For example: "relaxed and valued," "confident and cared for," or "heard and understood."

• Consider How You'll Set This Tone: List two or three actions you can take to reinforce this feeling, like offering a warm greeting, asking open-ended questions, or checking in regularly throughout the appointment.

Step 2: Outline Your Signature Consultation Routine

Your consultation is the foundation of the experience. Create a simple but effective routine that helps you understand clients' needs while showcasing your expertise.

• Build Your Consultation Questions: Write down 3-5 go-to questions that will help you understand your client's style goals, lifestyle, and preferences. These should be open-ended to encourage clients to share.

• Highlight Your Recommendations: Decide on how you'll offer suggestions. Will you use visuals, explain styling techniques, or point out how the cut will highlight their features? Think of ways to keep it personalized but efficient.

Step 3: List Your Key "Connection Moments"

Choose a few simple ways to make each client feel valued and connected. These small gestures will make your approach memorable.

• Choose 2-3 Connection Moments: Write down specific actions, like remembering personal details, offering a genuine compliment, or celebrating their style choice. These touches should feel authentic to you and enhance their overall experience.

• Commit to Consistency: Make it a goal to add these moments to every appointment. Whether it's remembering their preferred fringe length or congratulating them on a new look, these moments create loyalty.

Step 4: Develop Your Follow-Up Plan

Follow-up care shows clients that you're invested in their look beyond the appointment. It doesn't have to be complicated—just consistent.

• Create a Simple Follow-Up Routine: Decide if you'll send a quick message or email after big style changes, or if you'll check in at the next appointment about how they felt about the last cut. Make it a habit to stay connected.

• Offer Styling Tips or Maintenance Advice: Consider giving each client one or two easy styling tips or product recommendations to help them maintain their look at home.

Bringing It All Together

Your signature client experience is a reflection of your unique approach as a stylist. By defining each step, you're creating a consistent, personalized experience that clients will come to recognize and appreciate. This isn't just about creating repeat business; it's about building relationships and establishing your brand as a go-to expert who truly cares.

Make these routines a part of every appointment, and watch as clients become loyal supporters who value the full experience of being in your chair.

Wrap-Up and Next Steps

Creating an Experience Clients Remember

In this chapter, you've learned how to go beyond the technical skills and create a client experience that's memorable, personalized, and rooted in trust. From mastering the consultation to building moments of connection, each step is a chance to reinforce why clients choose you and come back for more. A signature client experience isn't just about delivering a great cut—it's about building a brand that clients love to be a part of.

By focusing on consistency, genuine connection, and small personal touches, you're giving clients more than just a haircut. You're offering them a place where they feel valued, understood, and confident in their style. Every appointment becomes an opportunity to strengthen your relationship with them, creating loyalty and turning clients into advocates for your business.

Next Steps

Now that you've mastered the client experience, it's time to focus on expanding your brand presence. In the next chapter, we'll explore how to elevate your reputation through the energy you bring, the expertise you share, and the way you present yourself. You'll learn how to make every interaction, from consultations to social media, reflect the quality and professionalism you bring to your craft.

Get ready to refine your approach and build a brand presence that goes beyond the chair, helping you reach even more clients who are looking for a specialist they can trust.

Chapter Four: Elevating Your Reputation Through Presence and Expertise

Embracing my career as more than just doing someone's hair was a journey that Kelly, a client, helped me see with new eyes. Kelly worked in corporate America, and during our appointments, she shared how my work inspired her. She admired the freedom and flexibility I had as an entrepreneur—advantages she didn't experience in her corporate role. Hearing her perspective opened my eyes to the unique position I held.

She told me that watching my journey sparked her desire to pursue entrepreneurship herself, to have access to the leverages she saw me enjoying. It was then that I realized my career wasn't just about offering a service; it was as if I had my hands on a honeycomb, a goldmine—a precious gift with the potential to impact far beyond the chair. As a Black woman in this industry, I began to see that the ceiling I faced wasn't a limit, but something I was meant to shatter.

Through Kelly's insights, I came to understand that branding wasn't just about how others saw me; it was about fully embodying who I am and the value I bring. My work held the power to inspire, uplift, and show others what's possible when they embrace the treasures of their own talent. This wasn't just my career; it was my purpose—a way to create impact, break barriers, and leave a legacy that goes beyond the salon.

The Power of Presence and Professionalism

Presence Shapes Perception

In the beauty industry, your presence speaks volumes before you say a single word. It's more than just showing up—your presence is about the energy, confidence, and professionalism you bring to each appointment. Clients are looking for someone they can trust, not only with their appearance but also with their time and comfort. A strong, confident presence tells clients they're in capable hands and reassures them that they made the right choice.

Your presence becomes part of your brand. When you carry yourself with confidence and approach each interaction professionally, clients associate these qualities with you and your work. They'll see you as more than just a stylist—they'll view you as an expert, a trusted professional who values quality and consistency.

Projecting Confidence and Approachability

Confidence is key to building a successful reputation, but it's essential that this confidence feels approachable. Clients want a stylist who knows their craft but is also down-to-earth and easy to connect with. Here are a few ways to find that balance:

- Maintain Eye Contact: Eye contact communicates confidence, honesty, and engagement. When you're talking with a client, eye contact helps them feel seen and valued, strengthening the connection and building trust.

•	Stand Tall and Show Pride in Your Work: Your body language says a lot about your confidence. Stand with good posture and move with purpose, whether you're styling, consulting, or simply interacting. When you carry yourself with pride, clients feel more comfortable trusting you with their style.

•	Smile and Stay Present: A warm smile and calm, focused energy make clients feel at ease. Even on busy days, a genuine smile shows clients you're glad to be working with them. Staying present reinforces that you're there to make their experience the best it can be.

Why Professionalism Matters in Building Trust

Professionalism isn't about being overly formal—it's about showing clients that you take your role seriously. Professionalism is reflected in how you communicate, how you respect their time, and how you maintain your workspace. When clients see that you're consistent in these areas, they trust that your work is dependable and that you're committed to their satisfaction.

•	Be Punctual: Respecting appointment times tells clients that you value their time as much as your own. When you're on schedule, clients feel like they're your priority and that their experience is important to you.

•	Keep Your Space Tidy: A clean, organized workspace signals that you're detail-oriented and take pride in your craft. Clients notice these small details, and a tidy station reinforces your commitment to quality.

•   Follow Through with What You Say: If you make a recommendation or offer styling advice, follow through on it. Clients remember when you keep your word, and this reliability strengthens your professional reputation.

Presence is Part of Your Brand

Your presence, confidence, and professionalism are all essential components of your brand. They're what clients see and feel when they sit in your chair, and they're what set you apart from other stylists. By cultivating a strong presence, you're not only creating an experience clients will remember—you're building a reputation that speaks to your dedication and expertise.

A consistent, confident presence tells clients they're with someone they can rely on, someone who's invested in their satisfaction and committed to delivering quality every time. This is what makes clients return, refer, and remember your name.

Building Trust Through Energy and Engagement

Your Energy Sets the Tone

The energy you bring into each appointment shapes how clients feel in your chair. From your attitude to your focus, every interaction sends a message about your professionalism and passion for your work. Clients pick up on your energy—whether it's calm, focused, or rushed—and it influences how they experience the appointment. When you bring a steady, positive energy, it reassures clients that you're fully present and committed to making their time with you a priority.

Your energy isn't just about how you act; it's about the genuine enthusiasm and pride you bring to your work. Clients want to feel that their stylist is excited to work with them and invested in their results. When you approach each appointment with a balanced energy, clients feel valued and relaxed, which builds trust and makes the experience memorable.

Staying Engaged and Attentive

Engagement is key to making clients feel that they're more than just an appointment on your schedule. When you're fully engaged, you're listening to their needs, responding to their questions, and showing that their satisfaction is important to you. Staying attentive during each appointment reinforces that you're committed to their experience.

•	Listen Actively: When clients are talking, give them your full attention. Avoid interrupting or letting your mind wander. Active listening shows clients that you respect their opinions and preferences, and it gives you valuable insights into what they're looking for.

•	Respond with Interest: Engage with what they're

saying, whether it's about their style goals or a story from their day. A simple "That sounds amazing!" or "Tell me more about that!" goes a long way in making clients feel that you're genuinely interested in them, not just focused on the cut.

• Stay Mindful of Non-Verbal Cues: Your body language speaks volumes. Nodding, smiling, and maintaining eye contact shows that you're engaged and interested. These non-verbal cues make clients feel heard and appreciated.

Creating a Calm, Positive Atmosphere

On busy days, it's easy to feel rushed or overwhelmed, but it's essential to maintain a calm, positive atmosphere. When clients sense calmness in your approach, it reassures them that you're in control and focused on delivering a great experience. Here's how to keep your energy balanced, even on the busiest days:

• Take a Breath Before Each Appointment: Give yourself a moment to reset between clients. A few deep breaths can help you center your energy and bring your focus fully to the next appointment. This small step ensures that each client gets your best, no matter how full your schedule is.

• Keep a Consistent Tone: Even if you're dealing with a challenging day, maintain a steady, professional tone. A calm, steady voice makes clients feel relaxed and comfortable, which enhances their experience and reinforces your professionalism.

• Focus on the Positive: When you exude positivity, clients respond. Show enthusiasm for their look, offer encouragement, and keep the conversation light. Positive energy is contagious, and it leaves clients feeling uplifted and satisfied with their experience.

Why Engagement Builds Trust

When clients feel that you're truly present and engaged, they trust that you're committed to making their time with you worthwhile. This trust is essential in building a long-term relationship, and it's what turns first-time clients into loyal customers who come back and refer friends. Your engagement and energy communicate that you care about them and their experience, not just the end result.

Clients who feel seen and valued by their stylist are more likely to open up about their style goals, share their honest feedback, and take your recommendations seriously. This kind of open, trusting relationship makes your job easier and ensures that clients feel confident in your expertise and approach.

Practical Tips for Keeping Energy and Engagement Consistent

Staying consistently engaged and energized requires practice and a bit of self-care. Here are some practical ways to maintain your focus and presence:

•   Take Short Breaks When Possible: If you have back-to-back clients, take even a minute or two to stretch or grab a quick sip of water. This helps you recharge and come back with full energy.

•   Set Intentions for Each Appointment: Before each

appointment, set a small intention, like "I'm going to focus on making this client feel relaxed" or "I'll pay extra attention to their style goals." Setting an intention helps you stay focused and engaged.

•   Keep the Conversation Client-Focused: While sharing a bit about yourself can create a connection, keep the focus primarily on the client. This keeps them feeling valued and ensures the conversation enhances their experience.

Engagement is an Extension of Your Brand

Every client interaction is a chance to reinforce your brand as a stylist who truly cares. Your energy and engagement communicate that you're passionate about your work and committed to giving clients a top-notch experience. When clients leave feeling that they were the focus of your attention and that their satisfaction matters, they'll remember that energy long after the appointment ends.

By staying fully present and engaged, you're not only building trust but also building a reputation as a stylist who values every client. This is what makes clients feel special and keeps them coming back. It's also what sets you apart as a true professional in your field.

Using Expertise to Educate and Empower Clients

Sharing Knowledge Builds Loyalty

When you educate clients, you're not just styling their hair—you're giving them the tools to maintain and appreciate their look long after they leave the chair. Clients rely on your expertise to understand how to manage, style, and care for their pixie cut, and the guidance you provide sets you apart as a professional who truly cares. Sharing knowledge builds loyalty because it shows clients that you're invested in their satisfaction beyond the appointment.

Empowering clients with the know-how to take care of their look at home strengthens their confidence in you and in themselves. They'll leave feeling capable, informed, and ready to show off their style, and they'll remember the experience as one where they learned something valuable. This isn't about overwhelming clients with information— it's about giving them just the right insights to feel confident and capable.

Educate Without Overwhelming

Your clients don't need a full tutorial; they need practical tips they can use. Tailor your advice to each client's experience level, lifestyle, and comfort with styling. Keep the tips simple, relevant, and easy for them to replicate at home.

• Focus on Basics First: Start with the essentials, like how to maintain volume or keep the cut looking sharp between appointments. For clients new to the pixie cut, explain how the shape works with their features and what maintenance will look like.

• Address Their Main Concerns: If a client mentions issues with frizz, flatness, or shine, offer solutions that directly address those concerns. Tailored advice makes clients feel understood and helps them see the value in your expertise.

• Keep Product Recommendations Simple: Instead of suggesting a full lineup, recommend one or two key products that make a big difference. If a client needs hold, suggest a light styling cream. For those needing volume, offer tips on using a root lift spray. Clear, focused recommendations are easy for clients to remember and apply.

Turn Routine Tasks into Teachable Moments

Throughout the appointment, look for natural opportunities to share insights. Whether you're sectioning, blow-drying, or finishing, these routine tasks are chances to explain why certain steps are important and how they can adapt them at home.

• During the Cut: If a client is watching closely, explain the techniques you're using. For example, "I'm adding some texture here to give your style more movement, which will make it easy to manage daily."

• When Blow-Drying: This is a great time to demonstrate how they can create volume or achieve a sleek look. Show them the direction and angle to dry for maximum effect, and mention any tools that would help, like a small round brush for added lift.

• In the Finishing Touches: When adding product, take a moment to explain its purpose. "I'm using this pomade for definition; it'll help you keep your style looking polished but natural."

These small explanations make clients feel involved in the process and give them confidence to recreate their look at home.

Empower Clients with Styling Tips and Tricks

Giving clients simple styling tips turns your expertise into something they can use every day. Tips that are easy to understand and apply are especially valuable for clients who want a low-maintenance look but still want to keep their pixie cut looking fresh.

- Tips for a Quick Refresh: For clients who are always on the go, suggest quick ways to revive their style. "Just a quick spritz of water and a bit of product can bring your volume back," or, "For a little more lift, try blow-drying the roots in the morning."

- Suggestions for Versatile Looks: For clients who like to switch it up, suggest easy variations on their pixie cut. Show them how to sweep their fringe to the side for a softer look or create a tousled effect with a bit of texturizing spray. This adds value by making the cut feel more adaptable.

- Maintenance Tips: Make sure clients understand the maintenance their cut requires. Explain the importance of regular trims to keep the shape, and suggest how often they should come in for touch-ups based on their goals.

Clients will appreciate these practical tips, and they'll see that you care about their satisfaction even after they leave the salon.

Why Education Strengthens Your Brand

When you educate clients, you're positioning yourself as an expert who's dedicated to their long-term satisfaction. This knowledge-sharing approach builds trust and sets you apart from other stylists. Clients recognize that your expertise goes beyond technique—you're invested in helping them feel confident in their look.

Educated clients are also more likely to become repeat clients. When they know how to style and care for their cut, they feel more connected to the look you've created, and they'll come back knowing you're a resource they can rely on. Each tip you offer, each product you recommend, reinforces your value as a stylist who's focused on their success.

Avoid Information Overload

While it's valuable to share knowledge, it's equally important to avoid overwhelming clients with too much detail. Focus on what will make the biggest impact and keep explanations short, clear, and actionable.

- Prioritize Key Information: Stick to one or two main points that are most relevant for each client. Avoid overloading them with techniques they may not need or products that don't fit their lifestyle.
- Gauge Their Interest Level: Some clients want to learn every detail, while others prefer a simpler approach. Read their

cues and adapt your advice based on their interest level, so they leave with tips they'll actually use.

•   Encourage Them to Reach Out: Let clients know they're welcome to ask questions after the appointment if they need more guidance. This lets them know you're a resource beyond the chair and gives them confidence to reach out when they're ready.

Empowerment is Part of Your Brand

Educating clients isn't just about sharing information; it's about empowering them to feel confident and capable. When you give clients the tools they need to maintain their look, you're offering them more than just a service—you're giving them confidence that lasts long after they leave the salon. This is what builds loyalty, trust, and a brand that clients can count on.

By sharing your expertise in a way that's approachable and actionable, you're setting yourself apart as a stylist who cares about the complete experience. Clients don't just want a great haircut—they want the knowledge and confidence to enjoy it every day. When you offer that, you're creating an experience they'll remember and a reputation that will keep them coming back.

Establishing a Consistent Brand Message

Defining Your Brand Message

Your brand message is the core of what you represent as a stylist. It's more than just a tagline or a set of services; it's the unique combination of qualities, values, and expertise that make clients choose you. A consistent brand message tells clients who you are, what you stand for, and what they can expect from every interaction with you. When your message is clear, clients know exactly why they're sitting in your chair and why they'll come back.

To define your brand message, think about what sets you apart. What are the qualities that clients love about working with you? What kind of experience do you provide that they won't find anywhere else? Your brand message should reflect the qualities and values you bring to your work and communicate them in a way that clients can connect with.

Clarify Your Core Values

Your values are the foundation of your brand message. They're the guiding principles that influence everything you do, from how you interact with clients to the standards you set for your work. When clients understand your values, they feel more connected to you and your approach. Here are a few ways to clarify your values and bring them into your brand:

- Identify What Matters Most: Think about the values that drive your work. Maybe it's professionalism, creativity, or client empowerment. Choose two or three core values that define your approach, and make sure these are reflected in every part of your business.

- Keep It Client-Focused: Choose values that resonate with your clients and align with their expectations. For example, if one of your values is empowerment, make sure that clients feel empowered through education, style choices, and your willingness to listen.

- Communicate Your Values Clearly: Whether it's on your website, social media, or in conversations with clients, make sure your values come through. Use language that reflects these values, so clients know what to expect from you and feel confident in your brand.

Craft a Consistent Message Across Platforms

Once you've defined your message, consistency is key. Your clients should see the same values, tone, and level of professionalism in every interaction with you, whether it's in person, on social media, or in written communication. Consistency builds credibility, making clients feel secure in their decision to work with you.

- Create a Brand Voice: Your brand voice is the tone and style of your communication. Are you professional and direct, friendly and conversational, or confident and polished? Decide on a voice that fits your brand, and stick to it in every message, post, and client interaction.

- Reinforce Your Message: Use language that echoes your brand values, like phrases that emphasize client empowerment, trust, or expertise. This reinforces your message and reminds clients why they chose you.

- Stay Consistent with Visuals: Your brand's visual identity—like colors, logos, and imagery—should also align with your message. Clients should feel a sense of continuity across all of your branding, both online and in the salon.

Be Clear and Transparent in Your Services

Clients want to know what they can expect from working with you, and a clear brand message helps them understand exactly what they're signing up for. This is especially important if you're positioning yourself as a pixie specialist. Clarity and transparency in your services make clients feel comfortable, informed, and confident in your expertise.

- Define Your Specialization: Be clear about what you offer as a pixie specialist and what makes your approach unique. Whether it's in your bio, service descriptions, or social media, make sure clients understand that you're focused on mastery in this area.

- Outline the Client Experience: Describe the experience clients can expect, from the consultation to the final styling. Let them know you're committed to providing a personalized, high-quality service.

- Be Transparent About Pricing: Clients appreciate

transparency when it comes to pricing. Clearly communicate your rates and any additional costs, so there are no surprises. Transparency builds trust, and clients will feel that you're upfront and honest in every aspect of your service.

Communicate with Consistency and Authenticity

Authenticity is what makes your brand message believable and relatable. Clients can tell when a message feels genuine, and this authenticity is what draws them to you. Make sure your message feels true to who you are and comes across as sincere, not forced.

• Stay True to Your Brand Voice: Whether you're posting online or speaking with clients, keep your communication style consistent. If you're naturally warm and conversational, let that shine through. Authenticity helps clients feel a personal connection to you and your brand.

• Be Consistent with Your Values: Actions speak louder than words. If you value client empowerment, ensure that every interaction reinforces this. If quality is important to you, make sure clients see this reflected in your work, communication, and attention to detail.

• Connect on a Personal Level: When appropriate, share a bit of your own journey, insights, or reasons for why you chose this specialty. Clients appreciate knowing the person behind the brand, and these small moments of connection make your message feel more genuine.

Your Brand Message is Your Reputation

A strong, consistent brand message is more than just words—it's the reputation you're building with every interaction. When clients understand who you are, what you stand for, and what they can expect, they feel secure in their decision to work with you. Your message becomes part of your identity, attracting clients who value your expertise and trust in your approach.

In the end, a clear brand message isn't just about marketing; it's about building trust, loyalty, and a reputation that speaks for itself. The more consistent and authentic your message, the more your clients will feel connected to you and your work. This is what makes your brand memorable, trustworthy, and irreplaceable.

Building Your Reputation Beyond the Chair

Your Presence Extends Beyond the Salon

A strong brand isn't confined to a single space—it reaches beyond the chair, influencing how clients see you both in and outside the salon. Building a presence that clients recognize and respect involves putting yourself out there, engaging with the community, and showing potential clients what makes your expertise stand out. A reputation that extends beyond your physical workspace reinforces that you're an established authority, trusted not only by clients but by the industry as a whole.

Every interaction, post, and event is a chance to share your passion for the pixie cut and your commitment to excellence. The more people see and hear about your work, the more they associate you with quality, professionalism, and expertise. Here's how to build your reputation outside the chair.

Utilize Social Media to Showcase Your Expertise

Social media is one of the most effective ways to reach a wider audience. It gives you a platform to share your work, connect with clients, and establish yourself as an expert in your niche. Consistent, quality content lets potential clients see your skills, understand your approach, and get a sense of your personality.

- Share Before-and-After Photos: Showcase your work by posting before-and-after photos of your pixie cuts. This highlights your expertise and gives potential clients a clear sense of the transformations you create.
- Offer Styling Tips and Product Recommendations: Use posts or short videos to share quick styling tips, product recommendations, or techniques for maintaining a pixie cut. This positions you as a knowledgeable resource that clients can trust.
- Engage Authentically: Reply to comments, ask questions, and engage with followers in a genuine way. Building relationships on social media makes clients feel like they know you, which strengthens their trust and loyalty.

Get Involved in Your Community

Building a reputation isn't just about online presence—it's also about showing up in your local community. Engaging with people in real life reinforces your commitment to serving clients personally, and it lets people see your passion and expertise firsthand.

- Host a Workshop or Demo: Offer a free styling demo or a workshop on pixie cut maintenance. This gives potential clients a taste of your expertise and lets them experience your approach without the pressure of a full appointment.
- Partner with Local Businesses: Consider collaborating with local businesses, like boutiques, fitness studios, or other wellness-oriented establishments. Partnering for events or promotions connects you with potential clients who value quality and personal care.
- Participate in Community Events: Attend or sponsor local events to increase your visibility. Being part of community activities lets clients see that you're invested in the area and helps you establish a reputation as a dedicated, trustworthy professional.

Network with Industry Peers

Connecting with other professionals in the beauty industry can also elevate your reputation. Networking with peers allows you to share ideas, learn new skills, and even gain referrals from other stylists who recognize your expertise in your niche.

• Join Industry Groups and Attend Events: Participating in beauty industry groups, forums, or local meet-ups gives you access to a network of like-minded professionals. These connections can lead to referrals and collaborations that enhance your brand's reach.

• Collaborate on Projects or Promotions: Partnering with other stylists or beauty professionals for events, giveaways, or special promotions can help you reach new clients while reinforcing your brand's position as a specialist.

• Invest in Continuing Education: Pursuing advanced training or certifications in your field strengthens your skill set and shows clients that you're dedicated to mastering your craft. Sharing these achievements on social media or with clients adds to your credibility and reinforces your expertise.

Your Reputation is a Constant Extension of Your Brand

Building your reputation beyond the chair is about creating a presence that clients recognize and trust, no matter where they encounter your brand. Each post, event, and interaction tells clients that you're committed to quality and passionate about your work. When clients see your name and work consistently associated with expertise, professionalism, and community involvement, it solidifies your position as a go-to stylist they can rely on.

A strong presence beyond the salon doesn't just build brand awareness—it builds credibility and loyalty. By reaching beyond the chair, you're not only expanding your client base; you're creating a lasting reputation that speaks for itself.

Exercise: Defining Your Brand Presence and Message

Turning Your Vision into a Clear Message

Your brand presence is what clients see, feel, and remember about you. It's the energy you bring to the chair, the expertise you share, and the way you make clients feel valued. This exercise is about getting intentional with that presence—defining what you want your brand to represent and how you'll communicate it consistently. Taking the time to articulate your message strengthens your brand, reinforces trust, and makes clients feel confident in choosing you.

Step 1: Identify Your Core Values

Start by getting clear on the values that drive your work. These values aren't just words; they're the foundation of every client interaction, every cut, and every recommendation.

- Choose Three Core Values: Think about the principles that shape your approach. Is it professionalism, empowerment, consistency, or creativity? Choose values that resonate with who you are as a stylist and what you want clients to experience.
- Define Each Value in Your Own Words: Write a sentence or two about what each value means to you personally and how it shapes your approach. This makes your values feel real and

specific to your brand, not just generic traits.

Step 2: Create Your Brand Message

Now that you know your core values, it's time to build a brand message that communicates them. Your brand message should be clear, memorable, and give clients a sense of what sets you apart.

• Draft a One-Sentence Message: Sum up your brand in one sentence that reflects your values and expertise. For example, "I help clients feel confident in their unique style by providing expert, personalized pixie cuts and empowering them with the knowledge to maintain it."

• Make it Client-Centered: Think about what clients value most. Center your message around how your approach benefits them, whether it's through quality, care, or expertise.

• Refine for Consistency: Use this message as a guide for all client interactions, social media posts, and branding materials. Consistency here will help reinforce your brand and make it recognizable.

Step 3: Define Your Communication Style

Your brand voice is how you speak to clients—in person, online, and in writing. It should reflect your personality while aligning with your core values and brand message.

• Choose a Tone: Is your tone professional and

polished, warm and conversational, or direct and empowering? Think about the impression you want to leave with clients and stick to it across all platforms.

• Practice Consistency: Review past posts or interactions to ensure they align with your chosen tone. Consistency strengthens your brand and makes your message clear.

• Adapt for Each Medium: Keep your voice authentic, but adapt it slightly based on the platform. For example, an Instagram post can be more conversational, while a website bio might be more formal. The key is to stay true to your brand message across every medium.

Step 4: Test Your Message

To ensure your message resonates, test it out in different interactions. Introduce it in consultations, use it in social media captions, and incorporate it into conversations. Watch how clients respond, and make adjustments if needed.

• Notice Client Reactions: Pay attention to how clients respond to your message. Are they engaged, nodding, or asking questions? Their reactions can give you insight into whether your message is connecting.

• Ask for Feedback: Trusted clients or colleagues can provide valuable feedback on how your message comes across. Sometimes, a fresh perspective helps you refine and strengthen your brand presence.

• Adjust as You Grow: As you evolve in your craft,

revisit and refine your message. Your brand will naturally grow with you, so make small updates to keep it relevant and aligned with your vision.

Your Brand Presence is an Ongoing Process

Defining your brand presence and message isn't a one-time task; it's an ongoing process that deepens with every interaction. The more intentional you are, the stronger and more recognizable your brand becomes. Clients will remember the way you make them feel, the values you bring to your work, and the confidence they gain from each appointment. By reinforcing your message consistently, you're creating a reputation that clients trust and return to again and again.

Wrap-Up and Next Steps

Summary of Key Takeaways

In this chapter, you've explored what it takes to build a reputation that clients remember, trust, and recommend. From the confidence you bring into the salon to the knowledge you share and the brand message you communicate, each step reinforces why clients choose you as their specialist. A strong presence, both in and beyond the salon, tells clients that your expertise goes beyond the haircut—it's an experience, a connection, and a commitment to their satisfaction.

By defining your brand values, crafting a consistent message, and creating a memorable experience, you're building a reputation that stands out. You've shown clients that they're working with a professional who values quality, connection, and long-term results.

Next Steps

With your brand presence firmly in place, it's time to focus on deepening client relationships and building loyalty. In the next chapter, we'll dive into strategies for fostering strong, lasting relationships that turn first-time clients into dedicated advocates. From personalized follow-ups to loyalty programs, we'll cover techniques that show clients they're valued and appreciated every step of the way.

Get ready to learn how small, thoughtful gestures and client-focused strategies can make all the difference in turning each appointment into a lasting connection.

Chapter Five: Building Lasting Client Relationships and Loyalty

One of the most important aspects of building lasting client relationships and loyalty is creating a strong first impression, and virtual consultations have become a key tool for me to do just that. These sessions allow me to connect with clients even before they step into the salon, offering a glimpse of who I am and how I approach their needs.

During these consultations, I get to see clients in their element, understand their energy, and hear their hair goals. It's often a conversation that uncovers not just their frustrations but also their dreams for their look. This initial connection isn't just about discussing technical details—it's about building trust and showing clients that I care.

By the time they arrive for their appointment, they already feel a sense of connection and confidence in our direction. This process taught me that loyalty isn't only about the results I deliver but also about the experience I create from the very first interaction. When clients feel valued and understood, they're more likely to return—not just for the service but for the relationship we've built.

Why Client Loyalty Matters

Loyalty is the Foundation of a Strong Business

In the beauty industry, loyal clients are everything. They're not only repeat clients—they're your advocates, the ones who spread the word, bring in referrals, and trust you enough to return time and time again. Loyalty is built on more than just delivering a great haircut. It's about creating a consistent experience, showing clients that they're valued, and making them feel confident in every visit.

Loyal clients are the ones who keep your schedule full, even in slower seasons. They're the ones who believe in you, follow your guidance, and understand your value. When clients feel connected to you, they're more likely to choose you over anyone else. Loyalty goes beyond business; it's about building relationships that last.

The Ripple Effect of Loyal Clients

Loyal clients don't just return—they bring new clients with them. When clients trust you, they're proud to recommend you to friends, family, and colleagues. These referrals aren't just random recommendations; they're personal endorsements, which means new clients come in already trusting your expertise. The ripple effect of loyalty can expand your client base naturally, without needing constant promotion.

- Loyalty Builds Referrals: When clients are happy,

they talk. Each recommendation strengthens your reputation and introduces you to clients who trust you from day one.

•   Consistent Revenue Stream: A base of loyal clients gives your business stability, making it easier to plan, grow, and offer the high-quality experience you're known for.

•   Stronger Client Relationships: Loyalty deepens the client-stylist relationship, making clients feel like they're more than just appointments—they're part of your brand's journey.

Trust and Loyalty Go Hand in Hand

Clients who feel valued are more likely to trust your advice, take your recommendations seriously, and feel invested in maintaining their look. Loyalty is built on trust, and trust grows through consistent, positive interactions. When clients see that you're committed to their satisfaction, they're willing to return even after trying something new or exploring other options. This trust makes the relationship stronger, ensuring that clients feel secure in choosing you for years to come.

In the end, client loyalty isn't just about keeping clients—it's about building a network of support, trust, and mutual respect that keeps your business thriving. A loyal client base is the foundation of your success, and every gesture that builds that loyalty is an investment in the strength and stability of your brand.

Personalizing the Client Experience

Why Personalization Matters

In an industry where clients have many choices, personalization is what makes your service memorable. When clients feel that their experience is tailored specifically for them, it strengthens their connection to you. Personal touches show clients that you're not just focused on their haircut; you're invested in their satisfaction, comfort, and unique style. This level of care builds trust and loyalty, making each appointment feel less like a transaction and more like a personalized experience.

Personalization doesn't have to be elaborate. Sometimes, it's the small, intentional details that mean the most. By taking a moment to remember a favorite product, ask about their preferences, or follow up after a big style change, you're letting clients know they're not just another appointment—they're valued individuals.

Ways to Make Each Client Feel Valued

Creating a personalized experience is about showing clients that you see them and that their time in your chair is special. Here are a few simple but effective ways to make each client feel valued:

- Remember Personal Details: Take note of the little things clients mention. Whether it's an upcoming vacation, a special event, or even a preferred product, remembering these details and mentioning them later shows clients you're listening and that their experience matters.

• Customize Their Recommendations: Each client's needs are unique, so tailor your recommendations accordingly. Suggest products, styling tips, or maintenance routines that align with their lifestyle, hair type, and style preferences. This personal touch makes them feel understood and valued as individuals.

• Acknowledge Milestones: Whether it's a birthday, a new job, or a major style change, acknowledging these moments creates a connection beyond the haircut. A simple "Happy Birthday!" or "Congratulations on your promotion!" lets clients know that you see them beyond the chair.

These gestures don't just make clients feel appreciated—they make them feel seen, and that's what builds loyalty.

Show Your Clients You're Invested

Clients can sense when you're genuinely invested in their satisfaction. When they feel that you're going above and beyond to make sure they're happy, it strengthens their trust in you and reinforces their decision to return. Here's how to show clients that their satisfaction is your priority:

• Check in Throughout the Appointment: Take moments during the appointment to ask if they're happy with how things are going. This makes clients feel comfortable expressing their preferences, and it shows them you're committed to getting it just right.

• Offer Tailored Styling Tips: At the end of each appointment, offer a few styling tips that are specific to their look. A quick explanation of how to add volume, keep their fringe looking sharp, or refresh their style in the morning gives them tools they can use, making the experience feel more personal.

• Encourage Feedback: Let clients know they're welcome to share their thoughts, even if it's something they'd like adjusted. Inviting feedback openly shows clients that you value their input and are dedicated to their satisfaction.

Follow-Up for a Lasting Impression

Following up with clients after an appointment, especially after a big style change, adds a final personal touch to the experience. A quick message or email lets clients know you're thinking of them and that you care about how they're feeling post-appointment.

• Reach Out After a Major Style Change: A quick "How's the new style feeling?" a few days after a big change can make a huge difference. It reassures clients that their satisfaction matters and that you're invested in their confidence with the new look.

• Offer a Quick Styling Tip or Product Recommendation: If a client mentioned struggling with volume or shine, follow up with a product suggestion or a simple trick that could help them at home. This small gesture reinforces that you're thinking about their needs, even after they've left the salon.

• Show Appreciation for Their Loyalty: A simple "Thank you for being a loyal client" message now and then can go a long way. When clients feel appreciated, they're more likely to remain loyal, recommend you to others, and continue returning for the experience you provide.

Why Personalization Builds Loyalty

Personalization isn't just about going the extra mile—it's about making clients feel genuinely valued. When clients see that you remember their preferences, tailor their experience, and follow up to ensure their satisfaction, they feel that they're more than just an appointment. They feel like they're part of something unique and meaningful, and that's what makes them want to keep coming back.

By building a personalized experience, you're creating a brand that clients can trust and rely on. They'll come to see your chair as a place where they feel cared for, respected, and valued. And when clients feel that level of connection, loyalty becomes a natural outcome.

Creating Loyalty Programs that Work

Why a Loyalty Program Adds Value

A well-designed loyalty program can do more than just keep clients returning—it can make them feel recognized, valued, and part of your brand community. Loyalty programs create a sense of exclusivity and reward clients for their commitment, showing them that you appreciate their choice to keep coming back. When clients feel that their loyalty is appreciated, they're more likely to stay committed to you, even when new options or trends come along.

An effective loyalty program doesn't have to be complicated or costly. It's about providing meaningful perks that show clients you're invested in their experience. A loyalty program tailored to your brand can deepen client relationships and help you retain clients in a way that feels authentic and consistent with your values.

Designing a Simple, Effective Loyalty Program

Keep your loyalty program straightforward and easy for clients to understand. A simple, clear program is more likely to attract and retain clients because they can immediately see the value. Here are a few approaches to creating a program that aligns with your brand:

- Punch Card System: A classic loyalty punch card offers clients a reward after a set number of appointments. For example, after five appointments, they receive a complimentary conditioning treatment or a small discount on their next visit. This system is easy to understand, track, and implement.
- Exclusive Discounts or Perks for Regular Clients: Offer a discount, early booking access, or complimentary add-ons for clients who book a set number of appointments per year. This approach works well for clients who value consistency and are likely to book in advance.

• Tiered Rewards: Create different levels of rewards based on how frequently clients visit or the services they book. For example, clients who come every four weeks might receive a larger reward than those who come every three months. This can motivate clients to maintain a regular schedule with you.

The goal is to keep the program simple yet valuable. When clients can see exactly what they're working toward, they're more likely to stay engaged and take advantage of the benefits.

Offer Incentives that Are Meaningful to Clients

The best loyalty programs provide perks that clients truly appreciate. Think about what your clients value most, and design your rewards to reflect those preferences. Here are some ideas for rewards that make a difference without undervaluing your services:

• Complimentary Services or Upgrades: Offer a complimentary add-on, like a conditioning treatment or a scalp massage, as a reward for reaching a loyalty milestone. These perks add value without taking away from your main services.

• Product Discounts or Samples: Clients often appreciate discounts on products they use regularly. You could offer a small discount on their favorite product as a reward for loyalty, or give them a sample of a product you know they'll love.

• Early Access to Appointments or Promotions: Reward loyal clients with priority booking or exclusive access to promotions. This creates a sense of exclusivity, making clients feel like they're receiving special treatment.

These rewards don't just feel like a bonus—they feel like a reflection of the value you place on their loyalty.

Balancing Rewards Without Undervaluing Your Services

It's important to design a loyalty program that feels rewarding to clients but doesn't compromise the value of your work. Avoid discounting your core services too heavily; instead, offer perks that enhance the experience without reducing your rates.

- Focus on Add-Ons Instead of Discounts: Rather than offering a discount on your main services, provide add-ons that enhance the client's experience. This could include a free treatment, a styling session, or a sample product. These add-ons add value without reducing your prices.
- Reward Referrals: Encouraging referrals through your loyalty program helps you build your client base while rewarding existing clients. Offer a small bonus or add-on service when they refer a friend who books an appointment. This keeps the program focused on growing your business in a way that benefits both you and your clients.
- Limit Discount Offers to Special Occasions: If you want to offer discounts, reserve them for special occasions, like client anniversaries or birthdays. This way, the discount feels exclusive and thoughtful rather than a regular part of the service.

A balanced approach keeps the focus on the quality of your work and reinforces that clients are receiving a valuable service, not just a discount.

Communicate the Program Clearly

Once you have your loyalty program in place, make sure clients know about it! Clear communication is key to getting clients interested and engaged.

- Introduce It During Appointments: When chatting with clients, mention your loyalty program and explain how it works. For new clients, it's a great way to encourage them to book their next appointment, knowing there's a reward system in place.

- Promote It on Social Media: Use social media to share details about your loyalty program. Highlight the benefits and explain how easy it is to participate. Visuals, like a simple infographic or video, can help clients understand the value of joining.

- Include It in Follow-Up Messages: After each appointment, consider adding a reminder about the loyalty program in your follow-up message. This reinforces the benefits and keeps clients motivated to continue booking with you.

A loyalty program only works if clients know it exists and understand its value, so make sure it's front and center in your communication.

Loyalty Programs Build Connections

A well-designed loyalty program strengthens your relationship with clients by showing that you're committed to their experience beyond the appointment. It's a way of saying, "Thank you for choosing me," while encouraging clients to stay engaged and keep coming back.

When clients feel valued and appreciated, they're more likely to remain loyal, refer friends, and see themselves as part of your brand's journey. In the end, a loyalty program isn't just about rewards—it's about building a community of clients who feel connected to you and your work.

The Power of Follow-Up and Check-Ins

Why Follow-Up Matters

A follow-up may seem like a small gesture, but it has a powerful impact on how clients perceive their experience. Following up shows clients that you care about their satisfaction beyond the appointment and that their style, comfort, and confidence matter to you. This connection keeps clients feeling valued and helps you stand out as a stylist who's truly invested in their experience.

Follow-ups also reinforce loyalty. Clients who feel appreciated are more likely to return, refer friends, and trust you with future appointments. When you reach out post-appointment, you're building a relationship that goes beyond just the cut—it's a commitment to their ongoing satisfaction.

How to Make Follow-Ups Personal and Genuine

The best follow-ups feel thoughtful and specific to each client. It's not about sending a generic message; it's about letting clients know you're thinking about their experience and are open to feedback. Here are a few ways to make follow-ups feel personal and memorable:

• Reference Their Recent Appointment: Mention something specific from their appointment, like a new style they tried or a product you recommended. This shows that you remember them as individuals and are genuinely interested in their satisfaction.

• Ask How They're Feeling About the Look: A simple "How's the new style working for you?" invites them to share their thoughts. This gives clients a chance to express any concerns, ask questions, or share positive feedback, all of which strengthen your relationship.

• Include a Helpful Tip: If you know they had questions about maintaining their style, offer a quick tip or remind them of a product they can use. This follow-up is both thoughtful and practical, showing clients you're committed to helping them feel confident in their look.

These small touches turn a follow-up into a moment of connection, reinforcing that you're invested in more than just their time in the chair.

Timing Your Follow-Ups for Maximum Impact

Follow-ups are most effective when they feel timely and relevant. Reaching out too soon can feel rushed, while waiting too long might make clients feel forgotten. Here's a guide for timing follow-ups to keep them impactful and client-centered:

- After Major Style Changes: For big transformations, check in within a few days. This gives them time to adjust and try styling it at home, so they can share genuine feedback.
- After First-Time Visits: New clients may have questions or uncertainties. A follow-up a few days later lets you thank them for choosing you and gives them a chance to ask questions they might not have thought of during the appointment.
- Before Regular Appointments: If a client hasn't booked their next appointment, a friendly reminder a week or two after their usual timeframe can encourage them to come back. Position it as a check-in: "Just checking in to see how your style is holding up—ready for a refresh?"

These timely follow-ups make clients feel that you're attentive to their needs and focused on their ongoing experience.

Building Connection Through Regular Check-Ins

Check-ins don't have to be reserved for after appointments. Staying in touch between visits helps maintain a connection and keeps you top of mind for clients. Here are some ways to check in that feel natural and client-focused:

• Seasonal Tips and Suggestions: Send a seasonal check-in with tips for maintaining their look during specific weather conditions. For example, you could share a quick message about keeping their pixie cut smooth and frizz-free during humid months.

• Product Recommendations Based on Their Needs: If a client mentioned a specific concern, like dryness or lack of volume, follow up with a product recommendation that addresses their need. This feels thoughtful and shows that you remember their preferences.

• Special Offers or Early Booking Opportunities: Offer loyal clients early access to promotions or priority booking around busy times. This not only shows that you value their loyalty, but it also makes them feel like VIPs in your brand community.

These check-ins keep you connected without feeling intrusive, making clients feel supported even between appointments.

Empowering Clients to Reach Out

While follow-ups are valuable, it's equally important that clients feel comfortable reaching out to you. Encourage an open-door policy so clients know they can ask questions, seek advice, or share feedback anytime.

• Invite Them to Ask Questions: After an appointment, let clients know they're welcome to reach out if they have questions about styling or products. This reassurance makes them feel supported and removes any hesitation to ask for help.

•   Let Them Know You Value Feedback: Tell clients that you appreciate their thoughts on the service and style you provided. When they know their feedback is valued, they're more likely to communicate openly and return with confidence.

•   Offer Multiple Contact Options: Give clients a couple of ways to reach you, whether it's by text, email, or direct messaging on social media. Offering flexibility makes it easier for them to get in touch in the way that's most convenient for them.

When clients feel empowered to reach out, it strengthens their trust in you and reassures them that they're in good hands.

Why Follow-Up and Check-Ins Build Loyalty

Thoughtful follow-ups and check-ins aren't just about staying connected; they're about building loyalty by showing clients they're valued beyond the appointment. When clients see that you care about their experience in an ongoing way, it reinforces that they're more than just another booking—they're an important part of your brand's community.

Clients remember these moments of genuine connection, and it's often the little things—like a quick check-in or a thoughtful styling tip—that make them feel seen and appreciated. By making follow-up a regular part of your client experience, you're not just maintaining relationships—you're building loyalty, trust, and a brand that clients are proud to recommend.

Encouraging and Rewarding Referrals

The Power of Client Referrals

Referrals are one of the most powerful ways to grow your client base. When a client refers a friend or family member, it's not just a recommendation—it's a vote of confidence in your expertise and a signal that they trust you enough to share their experience with others. Referrals help you build a network of clients who come in already feeling connected to you and your brand.

Creating a referral system shows clients that you value their loyalty and appreciate their support in helping you grow. When clients feel rewarded for their referrals, they're more likely to share their positive experiences, which naturally expands your client base in a way that feels organic and authentic.

Encouraging Referrals Without Pressure

The best referrals happen when clients genuinely want to share their experience, not because they feel pressured. Here's how to encourage referrals in a way that feels natural and client-focused:

- Make Referrals an Easy Topic: When a client is happy with their look, that's the perfect moment to mention your referral program. A simple, "If you have friends or family looking for a new stylist, I'd love to welcome them here!" can plant the seed without feeling like a hard sell.

• Highlight Benefits for Friends and Family: If your referral program includes a discount or incentive for new clients, let existing clients know. For example, "Your friend will get a complimentary treatment with their first appointment." This gives clients a reason to share the experience with people they care about.

• Express Appreciation for Word-of-Mouth Support: Clients who love your work often refer others naturally, so take time to thank them when you notice they've spread the word. A quick, sincere "Thank you for recommending me!" reinforces their impact on your business and keeps the connection strong.

These small nudges encourage clients to refer others without feeling like they're being asked to promote.

Offering Meaningful Rewards for Referrals

Rewarding clients for referrals not only thanks them for their support, but also strengthens their loyalty. Here are some effective and meaningful ways to show appreciation without undervaluing your services:

• Discounts or Complimentary Add-Ons: Offer a small discount on their next appointment or a complimentary add-on service, like a conditioning treatment, when they refer a new client. This adds value to their next visit without taking away from your core offerings.

• Exclusive Access or Early Booking: Give loyal clients who refer others access to early booking options or special promotions. This makes them feel like valued members of your brand community.

• Personalized Thank-You Message: Send a handwritten thank-you note or a quick personal message when a client's referral books an appointment. This gesture doesn't cost anything but leaves a lasting impression, showing clients that you truly appreciate their support.

Rewards should feel valuable but not overwhelming. It's the thought and personal touch that makes clients feel appreciated, not the size of the reward.

Celebrating Referrals Publicly

If clients are comfortable with it, recognize their referrals publicly on social media or in your newsletter. A quick "Thank you to [Client Name] for the referral!" gives them a moment of recognition and lets others know that you value client relationships.

• Share on Social Media: If a client refers a friend, post a shout-out (with permission). "A big thank you to [Client Name] for sharing the love! We're excited to welcome new friends to our salon."

• Feature in Your Newsletter: If you send a client newsletter, create a small section for referral shout-outs. This shows clients that their referrals don't go unnoticed and encourages others to participate in the referral program.

Public recognition adds a personal touch and builds a sense of community among clients.

Referrals Build Your Brand Community

When clients feel appreciated for spreading the word, they're more likely to refer others consistently. A well-designed referral program is about more than just rewards—it's about creating a community of loyal clients who believe in your work and want to share it with others. By making referrals feel natural, meaningful, and appreciated, you're building a network of clients who are proud to support your brand.

In the end, referrals are about trust, loyalty, and the strong connections you've built with each client. Recognize and reward those who help you grow, and they'll continue to bring in new clients who are ready to experience the same level of care and expertise.

Exercise: Mapping Out Your Client Loyalty Strategy

Building a Loyalty Plan That Reflects Your Brand

A strong loyalty strategy is about more than offering rewards—it's about creating a consistent experience that makes clients feel valued and invested in your brand. This exercise is designed to help you build a loyalty plan that feels natural, authentic, and aligned with the way you already connect with clients. By putting a plan in place, you're setting the foundation for deeper client relationships and ongoing loyalty.

Step 1: Define Your Loyalty Goals

Start by clarifying what you want to achieve with your loyalty program. These goals will help you shape a plan that's both rewarding for clients and beneficial for your business.

•   Consider Your Ideal Outcomes: Are you hoping to encourage repeat visits, increase referrals, or strengthen client relationships? Write down 2-3 specific outcomes that you want your loyalty program to achieve.

•   Think About Client Retention: How frequently would you like clients to return? If your goal is to build consistency, consider structuring your rewards to incentivize regular appointments.

•   Set Tangible Targets: For example, "Increase repeat appointments by 20%" or "Receive five new referrals per month." Clear targets help you measure the success of your loyalty efforts.

Step 2: Choose Loyalty Incentives

Now that you've defined your goals, select the incentives that will best encourage your clients to stay connected. Think about what clients appreciate most and how you can reward them without undervaluing your services.

•   Select a Primary Incentive: Decide on the main reward for your loyalty program, such as a complimentary treatment after five appointments or a discount for each referral.

• Choose Add-Ons or Bonus Perks: Consider offering additional perks, like early booking access, personalized thank-you notes, or seasonal styling tips. These small gestures add value and make clients feel special.

• Align Incentives with Your Goals: For example, if you want more referrals, offer an incentive specifically for clients who refer friends. If you want more repeat visits, focus on rewards for consistent appointments.

Step 3: Create a Clear and Simple Structure

A loyalty program is most effective when clients understand how it works and see its value immediately. Keep the structure straightforward and easy for clients to follow.

• Decide on the Milestones: Outline the milestones clients need to reach for each reward, like "Earn a free treatment after five visits" or "Receive a discount for every new referral."

• Establish a Timeline: Set a timeframe for earning rewards if necessary. For example, rewards might be available quarterly or annually to encourage ongoing participation.

• Keep It Client-Friendly: Use simple language to explain the program, and make it easy to join. A well-communicated plan feels welcoming and accessible to clients.

Step 4: Plan Your Communication Strategy

Once your loyalty program is in place, make sure clients know about it. Consistent communication reinforces its value and keeps clients engaged.

• Introduce It in Person: Mention your loyalty program during appointments, especially with new clients. A quick introduction makes them aware of the benefits and encourages participation.

• Use Social Media and Newsletters: Promote your loyalty program on social media and in your client newsletters. Share highlights, like upcoming rewards or client shout-outs, to keep the program fresh in clients' minds.

• Send Friendly Reminders: Include reminders in appointment confirmations or follow-up messages. A quick note about their loyalty status—like "You're two visits away from a free treatment!"—adds excitement and anticipation.

Step 5: Review and Adjust as Needed

A successful loyalty program evolves as your business grows and as you learn what clients value most. Regularly review your program's impact, and make adjustments to keep it relevant.

• Gather Feedback from Clients: Ask trusted clients for feedback on the program. Are the rewards motivating? Do they feel valued? Use their insights to refine the program over time.

• Track Participation and Engagement: Monitor how many clients are participating and if it's impacting your business goals. This helps you gauge the program's effectiveness and make data-informed adjustments.

•   Keep It Fresh: Consider adding seasonal rewards or special promotions to keep the loyalty program exciting. Regular updates help maintain interest and engagement.

Your Loyalty Strategy is an Extension of Your Brand

A thoughtfully designed loyalty program isn't just about rewards—it's a reflection of the value you place on client relationships. By putting a plan in place, you're building a client-centered experience that fosters loyalty, strengthens your brand, and enhances the sense of community around your business.

With your loyalty strategy mapped out, you're creating a structure that ensures every client feels valued and motivated to keep coming back. This connection builds a client base that not only supports your business but also trusts in the quality and care you bring to every appointment.

Wrap-Up and Next Steps

Summary of Key Takeaways

In this chapter, you've built a toolkit for deepening client relationships and fostering loyalty. From creating personalized experiences to setting up a referral program and mapping out a loyalty strategy, each step reinforces the message that clients are valued and appreciated. By focusing on meaningful gestures, genuine follow-ups, and thoughtful rewards, you're transforming each appointment into an experience clients remember and want to share.

A strong loyalty plan isn't just about keeping clients—it's about building a network of advocates who trust your expertise and feel connected to your brand. These clients become your greatest asset, supporting your business and helping it grow naturally through word-of-mouth.

Next Steps

With your loyalty strategy in place, it's time to focus on stability. In the next chapter, we'll explore how to create a consistent income through reliable processes that keep your business strong, predictable, and set for growth. From booking systems to client retention tactics, we'll cover strategies to ensure your income is steady and sustainable, so you can continue delivering the high-quality service your clients have come to expect.

Get ready to build the foundation that keeps your business thriving, bringing both financial security and the freedom to focus on what you love most—serving your clients.

Chapter Six: Systems for Stability—Creating Consistent Wealth through Reliable Processes

I remember the day I walked into another stylist's salon, hoping to enjoy the client experience myself. It had been a challenging day, and I was mentally and emotionally drained as I arrived. The stylist greeted me warmly, and after a brief pause, we started discussing my hair. I was in the mood for a cooler tone, but she kept steering me toward warm shades. Finally, I said, "Go ahead with whatever you think will work best."

Then came the budget conversation. Out came her calculator, and she quoted me $395. When I asked if she had a pricing menu, she replied, "I don't have my prices in writing, and I don't do anything for less than $225."

I felt my frustration rising. I'd always believed people in our industry would naturally value integrity and transparency. But here I was, facing a lack of both, and even found myself comparing her pricing to my own. I realized how far behind I was; my own prices hadn't changed in far too long, and I hadn't recently updated my client experience to reflect the value of my expertise.

At that moment, I knew I needed a realignment—my pricing, timing, and offerings all needed an upgrade. I'd let my value slip, forgetting how essential it is to create an experience and price that reflect the quality I bring to my clients. That experience reminded me that clear, competitive pricing isn't just a courtesy; it's essential for building trust, respect, and confidence in the value clients receive.

This moment became a turning point. I took it as a reminder to honor my expertise and deliver an experience that clients know is worth every penny. After all, when you truly value what you bring, others will too.

Why Stability Matters in Building a Thriving Business

The Power of Consistent Income

Consistency is the backbone of a sustainable business. When your income is steady and predictable, you have the freedom to focus on your craft, invest in your growth, and deliver a top-tier experience to clients without constantly worrying about the next booking. A stable income allows you to plan confidently, setting both short-term and long-term goals that align with your vision for growth and success.

Financial stability also provides a safety net, giving you peace of mind during slower periods. In the beauty industry, demand can fluctuate due to factors like seasonality, trends, and personal budgets. When you've built a foundation of consistent clients and predictable income, you can navigate these ups and downs with ease, knowing you have a reliable base to support you.

Stability Brings Freedom to Grow

A solid foundation isn't just about financial security—it's also about the freedom it brings to expand your skills, invest in new tools, or explore creative opportunities. When you have a stable business, you're less likely to feel pressured to take on clients or services that don't align with your goals. Instead, you can focus on refining your specialty, building client relationships, and shaping your brand in a way that feels authentic.

With stability, you're empowered to make decisions based on what's best for your business and clients, not just what's best for your bottom line. This freedom gives you the chance to pursue the clients and opportunities that excite you, creating a career that's fulfilling, rewarding, and sustainable.

Creating a Foundation of Reliable Processes

Stability doesn't happen by chance—it's built through reliable systems and processes that keep your business running smoothly. From seamless booking to consistent pricing and strong client retention practices, these processes give structure to your business, helping you create a dependable income flow that supports your vision.

Reliable systems also enhance the client experience, ensuring that every step, from booking to follow-up, is professional, consistent, and high-quality. When clients experience a smooth, predictable process every time, it reinforces their trust in you and encourages them to become loyal supporters of your brand.

Why Systems Matter for Client Satisfaction

Your systems don't just benefit you—they benefit your clients. A well-organized booking process, transparent pricing, and dependable follow-up practices make clients feel valued and respected. They know what to expect, they trust your professionalism, and they appreciate the consistency. This satisfaction strengthens loyalty, encouraging clients to book regularly and refer others.

In the end, stability is about more than income—it's about creating a brand that clients trust and a business that's built to last. By focusing on reliable systems, you're setting up a foundation that allows you to serve clients, grow your expertise, and achieve lasting success.

Streamlining Your Booking Process

Why a Seamless Booking Experience Matters

Booking an appointment is often the first impression clients have of your professionalism and brand. A smooth, easy booking process sets the tone for what they can expect from you and your services. When clients can book quickly, understand the policies, and feel secure in their choice, it builds their confidence and reassures them that they're in capable hands.

A well-organized booking system not only improves client satisfaction but also saves you time and reduces stress. It eliminates unnecessary back-and-forths, minimizes errors, and ensures that your schedule is always manageable. With a streamlined process, you can focus more on delivering exceptional service and less on administrative details.

Choosing the Right Booking Tools

The right booking system should be user-friendly for both you and your clients. Today, many online booking tools offer a range of features that make managing appointments easy and efficient. Here's what to look for when choosing a booking tool that fits your needs:

- Online Scheduling: Choose a tool that allows clients to book online. This convenience appeals to clients who prefer flexibility and enables them to choose an available time without needing to call or email.
- Automatic Confirmations and Reminders: Automated confirmations and reminders reduce no-shows and ensure clients remember their appointments. This also saves you the hassle of manually following up.
- Clear Service Descriptions: Ensure that each service in your booking tool is clearly described, with estimated times and prices. Clients will appreciate the transparency, and you'll minimize any surprises or misunderstandings during appointments.
- Mobile Compatibility: Many clients book appointments from their phones, so choose a tool that's mobile-

friendly. A streamlined, mobile-compatible interface makes it easy for clients to book on the go.

There are many booking tools available, so take the time to explore options, read reviews, and choose the one that aligns best with your needs.

Setting Clear Booking Policies

Your booking policies set expectations for both you and your clients. Clear, consistent policies help you maintain control over your schedule, protect your time, and ensure that clients understand what's required. Here's how to establish effective policies that reinforce professionalism and respect:

• Define Your Cancellation and Rescheduling Policy: Let clients know how much notice you require for cancellations and rescheduling. A standard policy might be 24 to 48 hours' notice to avoid a fee. This policy helps reduce last-minute cancellations that could impact your schedule and income.

• Set Up a Late Arrival Policy: Decide how you'll handle late arrivals and communicate this policy clearly. For example, clients who arrive more than 15 minutes late may need to reschedule. This ensures that you can stay on schedule and provide each client with the full attention they deserve.

• Confirm Your Deposit or Pre-Payment Requirements: If you require a deposit for booking, outline this in your policy and explain how it works. Deposits help secure commitment and reduce no-shows, especially for new clients or time-intensive services.

•   Keep Policies Visible: Display your policies on your booking page, website, or social media. Clients appreciate transparency, and having policies readily available helps reinforce that your time is valuable and that you run a professional business.

By setting clear policies, you're establishing boundaries that create a structured and respectful experience for both you and your clients.

Making Booking Simple and Intuitive for Clients

A straightforward booking process encourages clients to book confidently. When clients can easily select a service, pick a time, and confirm with minimal effort, it builds a positive first impression. Here's how to make booking as simple and intuitive as possible:

•   Organize Services by Category: If you offer a range of services, group them into categories, like "Pixie Cuts," "Color Services," or "Treatments." This organization helps clients find exactly what they're looking for without scrolling through an endless list.

•   Provide Clear Instructions: If clients need to know anything specific before booking, like bringing inspiration photos or allowing extra time for consultations, mention it in the service description. Clear instructions prevent confusion and make clients feel prepared.

•   Highlight Availability: Many booking tools show

your available time slots, making it easy for clients to see what works for them. If you're booked out, consider offering a waitlist feature that allows clients to fill any last-minute cancellations.

• Streamline Confirmation Steps: Keep the confirmation process simple. Once clients select a service and time, they should be able to confirm quickly. Avoid too many steps, and make sure they receive a confirmation message or email for reassurance.

An intuitive, user-friendly booking process ensures that clients feel confident and excited about their appointment, setting the stage for a great experience.

Why a Streamlined Booking Process Strengthens Trust

A seamless booking experience is part of what builds your reputation as a professional and reliable stylist. When clients experience an organized, smooth process, they're more likely to trust that every aspect of their appointment will be equally well-managed. This reliability fosters client loyalty, makes referrals easier, and reduces the likelihood of misunderstandings or cancellations.

In the end, your booking process isn't just a system—it's part of your brand. It reflects your attention to detail, your respect for clients' time, and your commitment to creating an experience that's both effortless and enjoyable. By streamlining booking, you're creating a foundation that supports a stable, thriving business and makes clients eager to return.

Setting and Maintaining Pricing Consistency

Why Consistent Pricing Matters

Pricing isn't just about numbers—it's a reflection of the value you bring to each appointment. When clients see clear, consistent pricing, it reinforces that you run a professional business where the quality of service aligns with the cost. Consistent pricing builds trust because it shows clients that they'll receive the same level of service every time, without surprises or last-minute adjustments.

Transparent pricing also makes it easier for clients to budget for appointments, plan for future visits, and understand the full value of what you offer. When pricing is consistent, clients feel secure knowing they're investing in quality and expertise, and they're more likely to view your services as essential rather than occasional splurges.

Setting Prices that Reflect Your Value

Pricing should reflect your expertise, the time you invest, and the quality of the experience you provide. Here's how to ensure your pricing structure is balanced, fair, and in line with your brand's value:

• Evaluate Your Experience and Expertise: Consider your years of experience, specialized skills, and client demand when setting prices. Clients understand that expertise comes with a premium, and pricing that reflects your knowledge and reputation reinforces your brand as a specialist.

•	Account for Time and Resources: Factor in the time each service requires, including prep and cleanup, as well as any products or tools used. Services that require more time and resources should be priced accordingly, so clients understand the investment behind each appointment.

•	Research Industry Standards: While your pricing should reflect your unique value, understanding industry standards can help ensure you're within a range that clients find reasonable. Look at similar stylists in your area with comparable expertise, and consider their rates as a baseline.

•	Align Pricing with Your Brand Position: If you're known for a luxury, high-quality experience, your prices should reflect that. Clients associate pricing with perceived value, so positioning yourself as a premium service provider can make clients feel they're getting the best.

Setting prices that accurately reflect your value reinforces your brand's professionalism and sets the foundation for client loyalty.

Communicating Pricing Transparently

Clients appreciate transparency when it comes to pricing, and a clear structure builds trust by eliminating any confusion. Here's how to make sure clients understand your pricing:

•	List Prices Clearly on Your Booking Page: If you have an online booking system, list prices for each service and any potential add-ons or upgrades. This way, clients know what to expect before they book.

• Be Upfront About Additional Fees: If certain services may incur additional fees (for example, extended time for complex styles or last-minute bookings), make sure these are clearly communicated. This prevents any misunderstandings and ensures clients understand the full cost.

• Discuss Price in the Consultation: For first-time clients or those considering new services, discuss pricing in the initial consultation. This sets expectations and gives clients a chance to understand the investment before they commit.

• Use Simple, Consistent Language: Whether you're talking about pricing in person or listing it online, keep the language simple and consistent. Clients appreciate clarity, and straightforward pricing makes it easy for them to plan confidently.

Transparent pricing strengthens the client relationship by showing that you value honesty, professionalism, and clear communication.

Adjusting Prices Thoughtfully Over Time

As your skills and demand grow, it's natural to adjust prices periodically. However, price changes should feel intentional and thoughtful, rather than sudden or arbitrary. Here's how to approach price adjustments in a way that feels fair to both you and your clients:

• Increase Prices Gradually: Rather than implementing a large price increase at once, consider adjusting prices in small increments over time. This allows clients to adjust to the new rates while recognizing the value you continue to provide.

• Announce Changes in Advance: Give clients notice of any upcoming price changes, ideally one or two months in advance. A simple message, like "Starting next season, we'll be updating prices to reflect new services and enhanced quality," helps clients understand the reasoning and plan accordingly.

• Add Value Alongside Price Increases: When raising prices, look for ways to enhance the experience. This could mean adding a complimentary add-on for loyal clients or upgrading the salon environment. Small gestures show clients that they're receiving added value as part of the adjustment.

• Explain the Reasoning: Clients appreciate transparency around price changes. Mention that the increase reflects growing expertise, improved quality, or additional investments in the salon. This reassures clients that the change is based on real value, not arbitrary decisions.

Thoughtful, gradual price adjustments show clients that you're committed to maintaining quality and value, and it builds their understanding of the expertise they're investing in.

How Consistent Pricing Supports Stability and Trust

Consistent, transparent pricing isn't just beneficial for clients—it supports the stability of your business. When your rates reflect the quality you provide, clients are more likely to value each appointment, return consistently, and refer others who seek a reliable, high-quality experience. Pricing that aligns with your expertise also sets a standard for new clients, reinforcing your brand's reputation as a trusted, professional stylist.

In the end, your pricing is part of the message you send to clients. By setting, maintaining, and communicating it thoughtfully, you're creating a foundation of trust that makes clients feel confident in the value they're receiving and secure in the investment they're making.

Building Client Retention Practices

The Importance of Client Retention

While attracting new clients is essential for growth, retaining your existing clients is the foundation of a sustainable, thriving business. Retention builds stability because it creates a base of loyal clients who return regularly, value your expertise, and spread positive word-of-mouth. When clients keep coming back, it means they trust your work, enjoy their experience, and see the long-term value in choosing you as their stylist.

Client retention isn't just about delivering great haircuts—it's about creating an experience that makes clients feel valued, appreciated, and understood. A strong retention strategy combines your technical skills with personal touches, follow-up, and incentives that show clients they're more than just an appointment.

Creating a Welcoming, Client-Centered Atmosphere

Clients who feel welcome and valued are more likely to return. A client-centered atmosphere goes beyond the technical service and focuses on creating an environment where clients feel relaxed, seen, and respected. Here's how to build a space clients want to come back to:

•	Offer a Warm Greeting: Greet clients by name and with a genuine smile. A warm welcome sets a positive tone and makes clients feel immediately comfortable.

•	Be Attentive to Their Preferences: Pay attention to each client's preferences, whether it's the style they like, the products they prefer, or even the way they like their coffee. Small details make a big impact, showing clients that you remember and value them.

•	Create a Comfortable Environment: Ensure your space is clean, organized, and inviting. A tidy, well-designed space helps clients feel relaxed, reinforcing that they're in a professional environment where their comfort is a priority.

These simple touches make clients feel appreciated and contribute to an experience that's more than just about the hair—it's about how they feel in your chair.

Personalizing the Client Experience

Personalization is one of the most effective ways to build loyalty. When clients feel that their experience is tailored to their needs and preferences, they're more likely to see you as someone who truly cares about their satisfaction. Here's how to make each appointment feel personal and memorable:

• Keep Notes on Preferences: If a client mentions a particular product, technique, or style preference, make a note. Referencing these details at future appointments shows clients that you're attentive to their unique needs.

• Offer Customized Advice: Tailor your advice based on each client's hair type, lifestyle, and preferences. Personalized tips on maintenance, styling, or product recommendations make clients feel supported and empowered to manage their look between appointments.

• Celebrate Milestones: Recognize birthdays, anniversaries, or other special occasions. Whether it's a small card, a complimentary add-on, or a simple acknowledgment, celebrating these moments makes clients feel special and deepens the connection.

When clients see that you're paying attention to them as individuals, they're more likely to return because they know their experience is uniquely catered to them.

Building Routine Follow-Up and Check-In Habits

Consistent follow-ups and check-ins are an essential part of client retention. They remind clients that you're invested in their satisfaction beyond the appointment and encourage open communication about their needs and experience.

•   Send a Follow-Up After New Styles: For clients trying a new style or significant change, send a quick follow-up a few days later. This gives them a chance to ask questions and lets you offer any additional tips.

•   Check In Regularly with Loyal Clients: Even if they're regulars, checking in between appointments shows that you value their loyalty. A simple message, like "Just checking in to see if your style is holding up well," reinforces that their satisfaction matters.

•   Remind Clients of Upcoming Appointments: For clients who book regularly, consider sending a reminder about their next appointment. This keeps them engaged and builds anticipation for their next visit.

Routine follow-ups reinforce that clients aren't just one-time guests—they're valued members of your client community.

Offering a Loyalty Program to Encourage Repeat Visits

A well-designed loyalty program can make clients feel appreciated and motivated to return. By offering perks for repeat visits, you're showing clients that their loyalty is noticed and valued. Here's how to create a loyalty program that feels meaningful and supports retention:

•   Simple Punch Card System: Offer a reward, like a complimentary treatment or small discount, after a set number of appointments. This classic system is easy for clients to understand and gives them something to look forward to.

•   Tiered Rewards for Frequent Clients: Create different reward levels based on visit frequency. For example, clients who visit every four weeks might receive a different reward than those who come every six weeks. This encourages consistency and recognizes different levels of commitment.

•   Special Offers for Referrals: Reward clients for bringing in friends or family. A small incentive, like a discount on their next service, shows appreciation for helping grow your business.

A loyalty program reinforces that you value clients' return visits and are committed to making their experience worthwhile.

Communicating Clearly and Consistently

Clients appreciate communication that's clear, consistent, and reliable. When they know what to expect from you and your services, they feel secure and confident in choosing you as their stylist.

•   Be Transparent About Policies: Make sure clients understand your policies on cancellations, rescheduling, and pricing. Transparency reinforces trust and helps avoid any misunderstandings.

•   Keep Clients Informed of Changes: If you're updating services, prices, or policies, let clients know well in advance. Regular communication shows that you're considerate of their needs and appreciate their loyalty.

•   Offer Scheduling Reminders: Encourage clients to book their next appointment before leaving, and send reminders to confirm. These small gestures keep clients on schedule and show that you're dedicated to maintaining a smooth, organized experience.

Consistent communication is the foundation of client trust, helping clients feel informed, prepared, and valued.

Why Retention Practices Support Stability

Client retention isn't just about keeping clients on your schedule—it's about building a foundation of loyal supporters who trust your expertise and value their experience with you. When clients feel consistently valued, they're more likely to refer others, book regular appointments, and invest in the services you offer. This loyalty creates a stable, predictable income flow, giving you the freedom to focus on growth, creativity, and continued excellence in your craft.

In the end, retention is about showing clients that they're more than just another appointment. It's about creating a lasting relationship that makes them feel connected to your brand and proud to be part of your client community. By implementing thoughtful retention practices, you're setting the stage for a business that's not only financially stable but also rich with meaningful connections.

Managing Finances with Confidence

Why Financial Management Matters for Stability

Managing finances isn't just about tracking numbers—it's about creating a foundation of stability that allows you to focus on growth and deliver consistent quality. When your finances are organized, you can plan confidently, invest in new tools, and set realistic goals without worrying about unexpected shortfalls. Financial management brings clarity to your income flow, helping you make informed decisions that support your business's long-term health.

By developing good financial habits, you're setting up a system that not only supports you during busy periods but also provides security during slower times. Consistent financial practices make it easier to budget, save, and grow with intention, ensuring that your income is steady and sustainable.

Tracking Income and Expenses

Tracking your finances is essential for understanding where your money is coming from and where it's going. Keeping accurate records lets you see patterns, recognize growth opportunities, and identify areas where you can adjust spending.

- Set Up a Simple Tracking System: Whether you use a spreadsheet, accounting software, or a budgeting app, choose a system that's easy for you to maintain. Track income from each appointment, and categorize expenses into areas like supplies, rent, marketing, and professional development.
- Record Income Consistently: Track each appointment, including any tips, retail sales, or add-ons. Consistent tracking helps you see trends over time and gives you a clear picture

of your overall income.

•   Monitor Expenses Monthly: Review expenses at least once a month to ensure you're within budget and to identify any unnecessary spending. This helps you manage your costs effectively and frees up funds for growth opportunities.

Accurate tracking provides the insights you need to make financial decisions confidently, ensuring that your spending aligns with your business goals.

Setting Aside Savings for Slow Periods

In the beauty industry, income can vary by season, with some months busier than others. Planning ahead by saving during peak times can help you maintain stability year-round.

•   Identify Peak and Slow Seasons: Recognize when your busiest months typically occur, and plan to set aside a portion of your income from those months. This ensures you have funds available during slower periods.

•   Create a Buffer Fund: Aim to build a savings buffer that covers at least a month's worth of expenses. This cushion gives you peace of mind and allows you to keep your business running smoothly, even when client demand dips.

•   Set a Savings Goal Each Month: Decide on a specific amount or percentage of income to save each month, especially during peak times. This habit helps build a consistent reserve that supports long-term stability.

Having a financial buffer reduces stress and allows you to focus on client relationships and growth, knowing you're prepared for fluctuations.

Budgeting for Growth and Development

Investing in your business is essential for continued growth, but it's important to budget carefully to ensure these investments support your overall goals.

• Allocate Funds for Professional Development: Set aside a portion of your income for education, courses, or certifications that enhance your skills. This keeps your expertise sharp and allows you to offer clients the best service possible.

• Plan for Marketing and Branding Expenses: Budget for marketing efforts, whether it's social media ads, website updates, or branding materials. Consistent, professional marketing builds client engagement and supports business growth.

• Factor in Equipment and Supplies: Regularly review your budget for equipment, tools, and products. Reinvesting in quality supplies ensures that you're delivering high standards to clients and that your workspace reflects your professionalism.

By budgeting thoughtfully for growth, you're ensuring that each investment contributes to your business's long-term success.

Financial Confidence Builds Business Stability

Managing finances with confidence isn't about perfection—it's about creating systems that make your income predictable, steady, and secure. When you track income and expenses, save for slower periods, and budget for growth, you're building a foundation that supports both stability and flexibility. This approach empowers you to focus on what you love—serving your clients and growing your brand—without the constant worry of financial ups and downs.

In the end, financial management is a tool that gives you freedom, confidence, and clarity. By keeping your finances organized and setting intentional goals, you're creating a business that's not only profitable but also resilient, sustainable, and positioned for long-term success.

Exercise: Crafting Your Stability Plan

Step 1: Define Your Income Goals

Start by setting clear income goals to give your stability plan direction. Knowing your target income provides a foundation for planning your pricing, client retention, and financial management.

• Set Monthly and Yearly Income Targets: Choose realistic monthly and yearly targets based on your current client base, service pricing, and average appointment frequency.

• Break Down Your Targets by Service: If you offer multiple services, estimate how much each contributes to your monthly goal. This helps you see which services drive the most revenue and may need focused marketing or upselling.

• Establish a Stretch Goal: Set a higher target that's achievable with consistent effort. This stretch goal provides motivation and highlights areas for potential growth.

Clear income goals give structure to your financial plan, helping you stay on track and make intentional business decisions.

Step 2: Build Your Client Retention Strategy

Retaining clients consistently is key to a stable income. Design a retention strategy that includes personal touches, follow-ups, and incentives to keep clients engaged and returning.

• Create a Follow-Up Routine: Outline a routine for checking in with clients after appointments, especially after major changes. Decide how frequently you'll follow up and through which channels, such as text or email.

• Design a Loyalty Program: Plan a simple loyalty program with rewards for consistent visits or referrals. Include specific milestones clients need to reach and the rewards they'll receive.

• Set a Booking Reminder System: Encourage clients to book their next appointment before they leave and send friendly reminders as their next service date approaches. This keeps clients on a consistent schedule.

An effective retention strategy ensures that clients stay engaged and loyal, contributing to predictable income.

Step 3: Establish Financial Tracking Habits

Tracking income and expenses is essential for monitoring your financial health. Set up a tracking system that's easy to maintain and provides a clear picture of your finances.

- Choose Your Tracking Method: Use a spreadsheet, budgeting app, or accounting software—whatever works best for you. Record income from each appointment, including tips and any product sales.
- Set Up Monthly Expense Reviews: Designate a time each month to review expenses and categorize spending. This keeps your budget on track and helps you identify areas where you can save.
- Allocate Monthly Savings: Decide on a savings goal each month, especially during peak seasons. Building a reserve for slower months keeps your income consistent and reduces financial stress.

These financial habits ensure that you're making informed decisions and creating a reliable income flow.

Step 4: Outline Your Marketing and Growth Budget

A stable business allows room for growth, so include budget considerations for marketing, education, and business investments.

• Allocate Funds for Marketing: Determine a monthly or quarterly budget for marketing efforts, like social media ads, website updates, or branding materials.

• Plan for Professional Development: Set aside a portion of your income for education and skill development. Continued growth keeps your expertise sharp and enhances your brand's value.

• Budget for Supplies and Equipment: Decide on a budget for tools, products, and other essentials. Regularly reinvesting in quality supplies ensures that you're delivering a high standard to clients.

Budgeting for growth allows you to make strategic investments that support both short-term success and long-term stability.

Step 5: Review and Adjust Regularly

Your stability plan should evolve as your business grows, so make time to review and refine it based on what's working.

• Set Quarterly Review Dates: Every few months, review your income goals, retention strategy, and financial tracking. Adjust based on trends and changes in client demand.

• Gather Client Feedback: Ask trusted clients for feedback on their experience, your booking process, or any improvements they'd like to see. This helps you enhance the client experience and maintain strong retention.

• Celebrate Milestones: Acknowledge when you reach income targets, retention goals, or financial savings milestones. Celebrating these achievements keeps you motivated and reminds you of the value of your hard work.

Regular reviews keep your plan flexible and effective, ensuring that it adapts to your business needs.

Your Stability Plan: A Foundation for Success

With a stability plan in place, you're creating a business that's financially secure, well-organized, and prepared for growth. Each step, from income goals to retention strategies, reinforces your commitment to building a brand clients trust and return to. This foundation not only supports your current success but also sets you up for a thriving, sustainable future.

Wrap-Up and Next Steps

Summary of Key Takeaways

In this chapter, you've built a comprehensive plan for creating stability in your business. From setting income goals and streamlining your booking process to establishing pricing consistency and tracking finances, each step supports a predictable and secure income. A foundation of stability allows you to make decisions with confidence, stay organized, and focus on delivering the high-quality experience your clients have come to expect.

By prioritizing consistent retention practices, financial management, and thoughtful growth budgeting, you're not only building a reliable income flow but also reinforcing your brand's reputation as a professional, trusted, and client-centered business.

Next Steps

With stability in place, it's time to focus on growth. In the next chapter, we'll dive into the Growth Mindset, exploring how ongoing development keeps your skills sharp, ensures that your expertise remains valuable, and builds a brand that's always evolving. From new techniques to personal development, we'll cover the importance of continued learning in building a career that stays relevant and rewarding.

Get ready to embrace a mindset of growth that enhances your expertise and strengthens the impact you bring to your clients and your business.

Chapter Seven: The Growth Mindset—Investing in Your Continued Development

One of my longtime clients, Ife, has always amazed me with her resilience and confidence. She navigates being a lady boss in a predominantly white corporate environment and leads social groups for Black women, all without missing a beat. I won't lie—I kind of crush on her. Pure amazement, right? One day, Ife came in, and her curls were different. They were sleek and smooth, and I loved the new look. She laughed and told me she'd gotten a smoothing treatment. We started talking about the stylist, and before long, I'd booked an appointment with her too. I don't mind giving props where they're due, right?

As we continued talking, Ife mentioned she'd been to Atlanta for a consultation to get Microlinks. She explained what they were and told me about the stylist who specialized in them. I started following the stylist on social media, fascinated by her work. Then Ife said something that gave me chills: "When I get them, I want you to keep them up." When I hesitated, she didn't. She just looked at me and said, "I know you can."

That confidence ran through me like a spark. I went to my mom's house that night, and together, we studied the stylist's Instagram late into the night. About a week later, I saw that she was offering a class nearby. It was a big investment, and with bills coming up, I brushed it off. But that night, Ife texted me, asking if I'd seen the post about the class. I couldn't bring myself to reply. I had already dismissed it due to a scarcity mindset.

At 3 a.m., I woke up thinking of something a client once told me: "You get to create the money." I'd seen this in action before; I'd even done it myself. Inspired by Ife's confidence and my client's words, I took action. By noon, I had the $1,600 for the class, which was in six days. That moment reignited a fire in me. Sometimes, all it takes is someone else believing in you to push past your own limits.

Why Growth is Essential for Lasting Success

Growth as a Cornerstone of Success

In the beauty industry, styles and techniques evolve constantly, and clients are drawn to professionals who stay ahead of the trends. Continuous growth allows you to adapt, refresh your skills, and offer services that meet clients' changing needs. When you're committed to learning, you're building a career that's flexible, resilient, and always relevant.

A growth mindset doesn't just improve your technical skills—it also boosts your confidence, enhances the client experience, and strengthens your brand. When you invest in your development, you're telling clients that you're dedicated to providing them with the highest quality service. This commitment builds trust, client loyalty, and a reputation for excellence that sets you apart.

The Benefits of a Growth Mindset

A growth mindset isn't just about mastering new skills—it's about seeing challenges as opportunities, staying curious, and embracing change as part of the journey. Here's how a growth mindset benefits you, your clients, and your business:

- Keeps Your Skills Sharp: New techniques and trends keep your expertise relevant. By consistently improving, you ensure that clients always receive a fresh, modern look that reflects current styles.

- Enhances Client Satisfaction: Clients love working with a stylist who's passionate about learning. When they see that you're knowledgeable and up-to-date, they feel confident that they're in good hands.

- Builds Confidence and Adaptability: Growth helps you face industry changes with resilience and confidence. Instead of feeling threatened by new trends or methods, you're ready to embrace and incorporate them in ways that align with your brand.

With a commitment to growth, you're creating a career that's both dynamic and sustainable, positioning yourself as a professional who clients can trust for years to come.

Why Growth Builds a Stronger Brand

A brand that's committed to growth is one that clients notice and value. When clients see that you're continually improving, they recognize the investment you're making in their experience. This commitment sets you apart as a professional who doesn't settle for the status quo—it shows that you're always looking for ways to enhance the value you offer.

In the end, growth is about creating a career that's built to last. By prioritizing your development, you're ensuring that your brand remains relevant, adaptable, and a reliable source of expertise for clients. Growth doesn't just add to your skills; it's a statement of dedication to your craft and to those you serve.

Setting Personal and Professional Development Goals (~750 words)

Why Goal-Setting Matters for Growth

Goal-setting isn't just about creating a list of things to accomplish— it's about shaping a path that keeps you motivated, focused, and aligned with what truly matters to you. Setting personal and professional goals ensures that your growth feels intentional and connected to the brand you're building. When you set goals with purpose, each step you take enhances both your skills and the client experience, helping you stand out in a competitive industry.

The right goals provide structure to your journey, giving you something to aim for and helping you measure your progress. They also give you a sense of accomplishment, showing that every effort you make is contributing to a bigger picture. Thoughtfully setting and balancing your goals allows you to focus on what brings value to your brand, your clients, and your personal fulfillment.

Creating Goals that Align with Your Brand

Setting goals isn't about trying to do everything—it's about choosing goals that reflect your strengths, your vision, and what you want clients to experience when they sit in your chair. Here's how to create goals that enhance your unique brand:

- Identify Core Areas of Growth: Think about the skills or areas that would have the biggest impact on your business and client experience. For example, if you're known for short cuts, a goal around mastering new pixie techniques would directly support your brand.
- Set Goals that Reflect Client Needs: Consider what clients value most. Maybe they love your creativity, or they appreciate your focus on client education. Set goals that allow you to deepen these qualities and bring even more value to your clients.
- Stay Authentic: Choose goals that resonate with who you are. Growth that feels authentic and natural keeps you motivated and allows clients to see the genuine passion you bring to your work.

When your goals are aligned with your brand, every achievement builds trust, loyalty, and a reputation for excellence that clients will remember.

Balancing Skill-Building, Mindset, and Self-Care

Growth isn't just about what you achieve—it's also about how you feel and the mindset you bring to each challenge. Balancing skill-building with mindset development and self-care ensures that your growth journey is sustainable and fulfilling.

- Focus on Specific Skills: Choose one or two key skills to focus on each quarter. This could be mastering a new technique, learning advanced color theory, or improving client communication. By focusing on specific skills, you're allowing yourself time to truly master them without feeling overwhelmed.

- Develop a Positive, Open Mindset: A growth mindset isn't just about gaining new skills; it's about approaching challenges with optimism and resilience. Set goals around strengthening your confidence, staying open to change, and embracing feedback as part of your journey.

- Incorporate Self-Care into Your Goals: Growth requires energy, focus, and balance. Setting self-care goals—like regular breaks, time for hobbies, or physical wellness—ensures you're taking care of yourself along the way. When you're well-rested and energized, you're better able to serve clients and stay motivated.

Balancing these three areas keeps your growth holistic and ensures that you're investing in yourself as well as your craft.

Setting Achievable, Measurable Goals

Goals that are too vague or ambitious can feel discouraging. Setting clear, realistic goals that you can measure helps you track your progress and celebrate each win along the way.

- Use the SMART Method: Make your goals Specific, Measurable, Achievable, Relevant, and Time-bound. For example, "Master two new pixie cut techniques within the next six months" is a SMART goal that's clear, focused, and realistic.
- Break Goals into Actionable Steps: Large goals can feel overwhelming, so break them down into smaller tasks. If your goal is to master a new technique, start by researching courses, then schedule practice sessions, and seek feedback from peers.
- Set Milestones: Create checkpoints along the way. These milestones allow you to measure progress and adjust as needed. For example, if you're focusing on improving client communication, a milestone could be receiving positive feedback on consultations within a set timeframe.

Achievable, measurable goals provide structure, making it easier to stay motivated and recognize the impact of your efforts.

Celebrate Each Achievement

Every goal you accomplish, no matter how small, is a testament to your dedication and growth. Taking time to acknowledge these achievements reinforces your progress and keeps you motivated for the next step.

• Celebrate Your Wins: Each time you reach a milestone, take a moment to celebrate. This could be as simple as treating yourself to something you enjoy or reflecting on how far you've come.

• Share Achievements with Clients: Let clients know about your progress, especially if it benefits their experience. For example, if you've completed advanced training, share it in conversation or on social media to build trust and excitement.

• Reflect on Your Growth: Regularly reflect on your journey and what you've learned. This reflection reinforces your accomplishments and helps you stay focused on your vision.

Recognizing and celebrating your achievements gives you the momentum to keep going, making each goal feel rewarding and meaningful.

Goal-Setting Drives Meaningful Growth

Setting personal and professional goals isn't just about achieving new skills—it's about building a path that keeps you aligned with your values, focused on your clients, and motivated by the progress you're making. By choosing goals that reflect your brand, balancing skill-building with mindset and self-care, and celebrating each accomplishment, you're creating a growth journey that's sustainable, rewarding, and uniquely yours.

With a clear plan in place, your growth becomes more than just a list of accomplishments—it becomes a reflection of the passion, dedication, and expertise that clients value and trust. Every goal you set and achieve strengthens your brand, enhances your client relationships, and brings you closer to the vision you're building.

Exploring New Techniques and Trends

Why Staying Updated Matters

The beauty industry is always evolving, with new techniques, styles, and tools emerging regularly. Staying current with these changes is essential for maintaining your relevance, demonstrating expertise, and providing clients with fresh options that meet modern standards. When you're knowledgeable about the latest trends, you position yourself as a stylist who's both skilled and adaptable, making clients feel confident in your ability to deliver the best.

Keeping up with industry trends doesn't mean following every fad—it's about recognizing what aligns with your brand and enhances the experience you're already offering. By being selective, you're adding skills that genuinely benefit your clients and reinforce your position as a trusted expert.

Choosing Trends that Align with Your Brand

Not every trend is worth your time or aligns with the brand you're building. The key is to choose techniques and trends that fit your specialty, resonate with your clients, and strengthen your reputation as a stylist.

• Evaluate the Fit with Your Niche: Think about your brand focus. If your expertise is in pixie cuts, for example, a trend around intricate braids or long styles might not be as relevant. Look for trends that align with your specialty, like new short-cut texturing techniques, modern color applications, or tools that enhance your existing skills.

• Consider Client Demand: Pay attention to what clients are asking about. If you notice multiple clients showing interest in a certain look or technique, it may be worth exploring. This way, you're meeting client needs while adding value to your brand.

• Stay True to Your Style: Choose trends that feel authentic to you. Clients trust you for your unique style and perspective, so if a trend doesn't resonate, it's okay to pass. Only adopt trends that you can incorporate naturally, making them feel like an extension of your brand rather than an add-on.

By carefully selecting trends that align with your brand and clients' interests, you're enhancing your reputation as a stylist who provides both quality and relevance.

Learning and Mastering New Techniques

Once you identify techniques that fit your brand, take time to truly master them. Learning a new skill goes beyond watching a quick video; it's about understanding the nuances, practicing consistently, and ensuring the quality meets your standards.

- Take Structured Courses: Invest in courses or workshops that teach the technique in detail. Look for hands-on classes or live tutorials where you can ask questions and practice under guidance. This ensures that you're learning the technique thoroughly and can apply it confidently.

- Practice with Intention: Set aside time to practice each new skill on models or mannequins before introducing it to clients. Focus on mastering the details, like placement, finish, and styling, so you can deliver the technique with confidence and precision.

- Ask for Feedback: Practice on trusted clients or peers and ask for their honest feedback. This helps you refine the technique, gain valuable insights, and build your confidence before offering it to a wider audience.

When you've truly mastered a technique, it becomes a seamless part of your skill set, enhancing the value you bring to clients.

Showcasing Your Expertise with New Trends

Clients love seeing that their stylist is up-to-date, and showcasing your knowledge of trends can spark interest and excitement. Sharing your expertise reinforces your brand's relevance and shows clients that you're invested in offering the best.

•   Use Social Media to Highlight New Skills: Share photos, videos, or even time-lapse clips of you practicing or performing a new technique. This not only educates clients but also builds anticipation and shows that you're always growing in your craft.

•   Incorporate Trend Education in Consultations: When a new trend aligns with a client's goals, offer it as an option during consultations. This reinforces that you're knowledgeable, creative, and ready to help clients achieve their ideal look in a way that's fresh and relevant.

•   Explain the Benefits: Whether it's a new technique for volume, shine, or texture, explain how the trend enhances the client's look. Clients are more likely to trust and try something new when they understand its benefits.

Showcasing new skills isn't just about self-promotion—it's about providing clients with options that enhance their style, giving them a reason to feel excited and invested in your expertise.

Balancing Trends with Timeless Skills

While trends are important, your core skills are the foundation of your brand. Balancing timeless techniques with selective trends creates a service menu that's both versatile and reliable.

•   Stick to Your Core Competencies: Don't let trends overshadow your strengths. For example, if you're known for precision cutting, make sure this remains at the heart of your offerings, even as you introduce new techniques.

• Adapt Trends to Your Style: Trends come and go, but your style is unique. Adapt new techniques in ways that reflect your personal touch, ensuring that clients can recognize your signature in every look you create.

• Focus on Quality, Not Quantity: It's better to master a few trends well than to offer a broad range with mediocre results. Quality always stands out, so choose the trends you're passionate about and dedicate time to mastering them fully.

A balanced approach keeps your brand both relevant and trustworthy, with skills that clients can count on year after year.

Trends Build Excitement, but Expertise Builds Loyalty

Staying current with industry trends shows clients that you're committed to providing fresh, modern options, but true loyalty is built on expertise and consistency. By selecting trends that enhance your skills and resonate with your brand, you're creating a service experience that's both exciting and reliable. Clients appreciate your adaptability, but it's the depth of your expertise and your dedication to quality that keeps them coming back.

In the end, trends add interest, but it's your unique skill set and authentic style that build trust and loyalty. By exploring new techniques thoughtfully, you're investing in a career that's both dynamic and deeply rooted in excellence.

Investing in Education and Networking

Why Ongoing Education is Essential

The beauty industry is one where change is constant, and clients expect their stylist to be knowledgeable about the latest techniques, products, and trends. Ongoing education keeps you sharp, ensuring your skills are not only up-to-date but also evolving to meet the needs of your clients. Each new course or workshop is an opportunity to refine your craft, discover fresh approaches, and bring something unique to the table.

Education is more than just skill-building; it's a commitment to excellence. By investing in your learning, you're showing clients that you're dedicated to their satisfaction and confident enough to keep pushing yourself. This dedication builds trust, reinforces your reputation, and sets you apart as a stylist who's always striving to deliver the best.

Choosing Education that Adds Real Value

With so many courses, workshops, and certifications available, it's essential to be selective. Choose education that aligns with your brand, enhances your current skills, and genuinely adds value to your client offerings.

- Prioritize Skills That Support Your Specialty: Focus on courses that deepen your expertise in your niche. If you specialize in pixie cuts, for example, advanced texturizing or precision cutting courses may be more valuable than broader classes. Staying focused on your specialty keeps your skills sharp and aligned with the brand you're building.

•   Look for Hands-On Training: Whenever possible, opt for hands-on courses. Practical experience builds confidence, allows you to practice under guidance, and helps you master the details. In-person or live virtual workshops offer a chance for immediate feedback, making the learning experience more immersive and impactful.

•   Seek Out Industry-Leading Instructors: Learn from the best in the field. Look for educators who have a strong reputation, years of experience, or a unique approach that resonates with you. The quality of your teacher can make all the difference in how deeply you absorb and apply new skills.

When your education choices are aligned with your goals, each course feels like a stepping stone, bringing you closer to the vision you have for your brand and career.

Exploring New Horizons Beyond Technical Skills

Education isn't just about mastering techniques—it's also about developing the qualities that make you a well-rounded, resilient professional. Building skills in areas like client communication, time management, or even business strategy can support your growth in ways that go beyond the chair.

• Consider Courses in Client Communication: Mastering communication improves every aspect of the client experience. Courses that focus on consultation skills, active listening, or handling feedback can make you a more effective and empathetic stylist, helping you build stronger connections.

• Invest in Business Skills: Running a successful salon or freelance business requires more than technical skills. Learning about budgeting, marketing, or social media strategy can help you manage your business with confidence and create a brand that clients recognize and trust.

• Explore Mindset and Self-Care Workshops: The right mindset is essential for growth and sustainability. Mindset workshops, meditation, or self-care retreats can provide the tools to handle stress, stay positive, and keep your passion for the industry alive.

A well-rounded education supports both your technical skills and your personal growth, helping you build a career that's fulfilling, balanced, and sustainable.

Building a Network That Inspires and Supports You

Networking isn't just about making contacts—it's about creating a support system of peers, mentors, and industry professionals who inspire and motivate you. A strong network keeps you connected, offers fresh perspectives, and provides a sense of community in an industry that can sometimes feel isolating.

• Join Industry Groups and Associations: Industry organizations offer resources, events, and a network of professionals who share your passion. Being part of a group allows you to stay updated on industry standards, connect with other stylists, and access continuing education opportunities.

• Attend Conferences and Trade Shows: Conferences and trade shows provide hands-on experience with new products, tools, and techniques. They also give you a chance to meet other professionals, learn from industry leaders, and feel energized by the community around you.

• Participate in Online Communities: Social media groups, forums, or online education platforms can connect you with stylists around the world. These communities allow you to share ideas, seek advice, and find inspiration. Even though they're virtual, these connections are valuable for staying informed and motivated.

Networking provides a foundation of support and inspiration, allowing you to continue growing in a way that's connected to the larger industry community.

Seeking Out Mentorship for Deeper Growth

A mentor can be one of the most valuable resources in your journey, offering insights, guidance, and encouragement based on their own experiences. A good mentor relationship provides perspective and support as you navigate challenges, set goals, and refine your skills.

• Look for a Mentor with Aligned Values: Choose

someone whose values and approach to the industry resonate with you. A mentor who shares your dedication to client care, education, or creativity can provide guidance that feels both relatable and motivating.

• Reach Out with Specific Goals in Mind: When approaching a potential mentor, be clear about your goals. Whether you want to improve a specific skill, learn about the business side of styling, or find guidance on work-life balance, having a clear purpose makes the mentorship more impactful.

• Be Open to Constructive Feedback: A mentor's role is to help you grow, which often means providing honest, constructive feedback. Approach mentorship with an open mind and a willingness to learn from both successes and challenges.

Mentorship is a powerful way to accelerate your growth, providing a trusted perspective that helps you stay aligned with your vision while pushing you to reach new heights.

Investing in Education and Networking Fuels Your Brand

Education and networking are long-term investments that bring depth, resilience, and creativity to your career. By continuously learning, you're showing clients that you're committed to excellence, staying informed, and always ready to offer the best. Networking connects you with a community of professionals who understand your journey, share your passion, and support your growth.

In the end, each course, workshop, and connection brings something valuable to your brand. These investments not only enhance your technical skills but also build a network and mindset that keep you inspired and motivated. With a commitment to education and a strong support system, you're setting up a career that's dynamic, client-centered, and ready for the future.

Exercise: Crafting Your Development Plan

Step 1: Define Your Development Goals

Start by setting clear goals for your growth. These goals should reflect the skills, knowledge, and personal qualities you want to develop, aligned with the vision you have for your brand.

• Identify Key Skills to Strengthen: Think about the skills that would make the biggest impact on your business and client experience. For example, mastering a new cutting technique, improving color applications, or enhancing your client consultation skills.

• Set Goals for Personal Growth: Consider areas beyond technical skills, like improving client communication, building confidence, or developing a growth mindset. These personal goals contribute to a well-rounded, resilient brand.

• Outline Your Timeline: Decide on a timeline for achieving each goal. For example, "Attend a color technique workshop within the next six months" or "Improve consultation skills by incorporating new methods over the next quarter."

Clear, intentional goals give structure to your development plan and keep you focused on what will truly enhance your brand and client experience.

Step 2: Choose Educational Resources and Opportunities

Once you have your goals in place, identify the resources that will support your learning. Look for courses, workshops, or mentors that align with your vision and will help you achieve each goal effectively.

- Select Hands-On Workshops for Key Techniques: If you're focused on mastering a specific skill, prioritize hands-on workshops. Look for in-person or live virtual options where you can practice, ask questions, and get immediate feedback.
- Find Online Courses for Flexible Learning: Online courses are great for skills that don't require live practice, like client communication or business management. Choose courses with reputable instructors and high-quality materials.
- Seek Out Mentorship: If you're aiming to grow in areas like business strategy or mindset, look for mentors who can provide guidance based on their experience. Reach out with clear goals to make the mentorship relationship valuable and focused.

By choosing resources that directly support your goals, you're making sure each learning opportunity brings value to your journey.

Step 3: Create a Schedule for Consistent Progress

Consistency is key to growth, so set up a schedule that allows you to make steady progress without feeling overwhelmed. Break down your goals into smaller tasks and add them to your weekly or monthly schedule.

- Set Weekly or Monthly Learning Milestones: For each goal, create specific milestones, like completing one module of a course per week or practicing a new technique twice a month. These smaller goals keep you on track and help you see tangible progress.
- Balance Learning with Practice: Plan time to practice new skills in addition to studying. If you're learning a new technique, schedule dedicated practice sessions with models or mannequins to reinforce what you've learned.
- Allocate Time for Reflection: Include time for reflecting on your progress. At the end of each month, review what you've learned, what's working well, and any areas you'd like to improve. This reflection helps you adjust your plan and stay focused on meaningful growth.

A structured schedule ensures that your development plan feels manageable and keeps you engaged with each step.

Step 4: Track Your Achievements and Celebrate Progress

Recognizing each milestone reinforces your growth and keeps you motivated. Tracking your achievements also shows you how far you've come, reminding you of the value of each investment in your journey.

• Record Key Achievements: Keep a journal or digital log where you record your accomplishments, such as completing a workshop, mastering a new technique, or receiving positive client feedback. This record highlights your progress and builds confidence.

• Celebrate Each Milestone: Take time to celebrate each achievement, no matter how small. Treat yourself, share your progress with clients, or reflect on how each milestone is bringing you closer to your goals.

• Use Your Achievements to Inspire Clients: When appropriate, share your growth journey with clients, whether through social media, newsletters, or in-person conversations. Showing your dedication to learning builds trust and excitement among clients who value your commitment to quality.

Celebrating progress keeps you energized and reinforces the impact your growth has on both your brand and client relationships.

Your Development Plan: A Roadmap for Growth

With a clear development plan in place, you're setting up a structured, intentional path to achieve your growth goals. Each step, from defining your skills to tracking your achievements, ensures that your learning journey is organized, meaningful, and aligned with the brand you're building.

This plan not only strengthens your expertise but also enhances the client experience, showing clients that they're working with a stylist who's passionate, dedicated, and always striving for excellence. With your development plan as a guide, you're building a career that's dynamic, fulfilling, and built to last.

Wrap-Up and Next Steps

Summary of Key Takeaways

In this chapter, you've established a mindset of continuous growth and developed a framework for ongoing development. From setting personal and professional goals to choosing the right education, building a supportive network, and crafting a structured development plan, each step reinforces your commitment to excellence. By prioritizing education, seeking inspiration, and staying connected with industry changes, you're creating a career that's resilient, adaptable, and always client-centered.

A growth mindset doesn't just improve your skills; it deepens your brand's impact, strengthens client trust, and builds a reputation for quality that clients recognize and return to. With this mindset in place, you're prepared to thrive and grow in an industry that's constantly evolving.

Next Steps

With your growth plan underway, it's time to focus on overcoming the challenges that come with building a specialized career. In the next chapter, we'll dive into Navigating Challenges: Turning Obstacles into Opportunities, exploring ways to handle setbacks like burnout, industry trends, and client demands. You'll learn strategies to stay focused, resilient, and motivated, turning every challenge into a chance for growth.

Get ready to approach obstacles with confidence, knowing that each challenge brings new insights and opportunities for your brand to shine.

CHAPTER EIGHT: NAVIGATING CHALLENGES—TURNING OBSTACLES INTO OPPORTUNITIES

In the early days of my career, there were times when I'd step outside my usual services, taking on requests that didn't align with my strengths or the processes I'd carefully built. Every time I did, it left me feeling unsettled. I'd rush through because I didn't have the right products, wasn't in the right mindset, or simply hadn't prepared for that type of service. The result? Sometimes I'd lose a client or feel I'd compromised the quality of my work.

Facing these uncomfortable moments made me realize that setting boundaries wasn't about limiting my services—it was about preserving the quality of what I offered. Sitting with these realizations, I learned to stand by the decisions I'd made around my specialties. I became intentional about what I offered, knowing that clear boundaries prepared me to give each client my best.

Through these challenges, I turned discomfort into strength. Establishing boundaries allowed me to bring integrity and consistency into my work. Now, every client leaves my chair with an experience I'm proud of, and every day feels purposeful, allowing me to build relationships that truly last.

Why Resilience is Essential for Success

The Power of Resilience in the Beauty Industry

The beauty industry is fast-paced and ever-evolving, and resilience is one of the most valuable traits you can cultivate to thrive in this environment. Resilience allows you to adapt to change, handle setbacks, and stay focused on your goals despite challenges. When you're resilient, you're able to face each obstacle with a problem-solving mindset, viewing challenges not as roadblocks but as opportunities for growth.

A resilient mindset isn't about avoiding difficulties—it's about embracing them with confidence, knowing that every challenge has the potential to strengthen your skills and your brand. By building resilience, you're creating a career that can weather ups and downs, navigate changes, and stay aligned with the values that make your brand unique.

How Resilience Strengthens Your Brand

Resilience isn't just a personal trait; it's a quality that impacts your entire brand. When clients see that you handle challenges with grace and confidence, it reinforces their trust in you. Resilience shows clients that you're reliable, adaptable, and committed to delivering quality no matter the circumstances.

- Consistency Under Pressure: Resilience helps you

stay consistent, even in stressful situations. This consistency reassures clients, making them feel confident that they can rely on you to deliver the experience they expect.

• Openness to Growth: A resilient mindset keeps you open to growth, encouraging you to learn from setbacks and refine your skills. Clients value a stylist who is always improving and willing to embrace change.

• Inspiring Client Confidence: When clients see that you handle challenges with positivity and determination, they're more likely to feel comfortable and inspired in your chair. Your resilience becomes a source of strength that they recognize and appreciate.

Resilience isn't about perfection—it's about showing up with a strong, solution-oriented mindset that keeps your business moving forward, no matter what.

Why a Positive, Solution-Oriented Mindset Matters

In the face of challenges, a positive, solution-oriented mindset allows you to focus on finding answers rather than getting stuck in the problem. By shifting your focus to solutions, you're actively building resilience, creating a brand that's proactive, flexible, and always moving forward.

This mindset empowers you to approach each challenge with creativity and optimism. Instead of seeing obstacles as setbacks, you're able to reframe them as opportunities for improvement, growth, and learning. A positive approach not only reduces stress but also makes the journey more rewarding, helping you maintain your passion, motivation, and commitment to your craft.

In the end, resilience is about more than enduring—it's about embracing each challenge as part of the journey, knowing that every obstacle can bring you closer to the brand you envision. With resilience as a foundation, you're building a business that's equipped to handle whatever comes your way.

Managing Burnout and Staying Inspired

Why Burnout Happens and How to Recognize It

Burnout is a common challenge in any high-energy profession, and it's especially prevalent in the beauty industry, where you're constantly giving your time, attention, and creativity to each client. Long hours, back-to-back appointments, and the physical demands of styling can take a toll. Burnout doesn't happen overnight—it's a gradual process that can creep up when we're overly focused on doing everything perfectly and meeting every demand.

Recognizing the signs of burnout is essential for staying healthy and motivated. Some early signs include feeling exhausted even after a full night's sleep, losing enthusiasm for tasks that once excited you, or feeling detached from your work. By being mindful of these signs, you can take action early, before burnout takes a toll on your passion and energy.

Setting Boundaries to Protect Your Energy

Boundaries are essential for preventing burnout and creating a career that's both fulfilling and sustainable. When you set clear boundaries around your time and energy, you're giving yourself the space you need to recharge and show up fully for each client.

- Define Your Work Hours: Set specific work hours and stick to them. If you've chosen to work three days a week, for example, avoid taking extra appointments on your days off. Clear boundaries protect your personal time, allowing you to rest and recharge.
- Limit Back-to-Back Appointments: Give yourself small breaks between clients. Even a 10-minute pause to breathe, stretch, or grab a snack can make a difference in maintaining your energy throughout the day.
- Create a Transition Ritual: When your workday is over, create a small ritual to transition out of work mode, like taking a short walk or enjoying a cup of tea. This helps you shift your focus and separate your work life from your personal time.

By setting boundaries, you're not only protecting your well-being—you're also ensuring that each client gets the best of you, every time.

Finding Inspiration to Stay Engaged and Motivated

Passion is what drives you in this industry, but staying inspired requires intention. Finding new sources of inspiration keeps your work fresh, makes each day exciting, and reminds you why you fell in love with this craft in the first place.

- Explore New Techniques and Trends: Learning new skills can reignite your creativity. Attend workshops, follow stylists whose work inspires you, or set aside time each month to practice a new technique. Fresh challenges keep you engaged and remind you of the endless possibilities in your craft.
- Take Creative Breaks: Step away from your routine once in a while to recharge. Visit an art gallery, attend a fashion show, or spend a day exploring nature. These breaks stimulate creativity and offer fresh perspectives that you can bring back to your work.
- Connect with Other Stylists: Talking with peers, sharing ideas, and learning from others' experiences can be incredibly motivating. Join stylist groups, attend networking events, or even schedule a coffee chat with a friend in the industry. A sense of community reminds you that you're not alone on this journey.

Inspiration fuels your passion, keeping each day exciting and allowing you to approach your work with renewed energy.

Embracing Self-Care as Part of Your Routine

Self-care isn't a luxury—it's a necessity, especially when you're giving so much of yourself to your clients. Embracing self-care as part of your daily routine helps you stay grounded, focused, and energized, making it easier to show up as your best self.

• Prioritize Physical Health: Regular movement, stretching, and a balanced diet go a long way in preventing burnout. Consider incorporating quick stretches during the day to relieve tension, or set aside time for exercise that you enjoy.

• Nourish Your Mind and Spirit: Self-care goes beyond the physical. Activities like journaling, meditating, or practicing gratitude can keep you mentally centered. Spending a few minutes each day to reflect or unwind helps you recharge on a deeper level.

• Schedule Downtime: Make time each week for activities that bring you joy outside of work. Whether it's reading, cooking, or spending time with loved ones, downtime is essential for maintaining balance and avoiding burnout.

When self-care is part of your routine, you're creating a sustainable way to manage the demands of your work without feeling overwhelmed.

Rediscovering Your "Why"

Sometimes, burnout happens because we lose touch with the deeper purpose behind what we do. Taking time to reconnect with your "why"—the reason you became a stylist and what you love about your craft—can reignite your passion and remind you of the impact you're making.

• Reflect on Your Journey: Look back on how far you've come, the skills you've mastered, and the clients you've helped. Celebrate your achievements and recognize the hard work you've put in to build your career.

• Visualize Your Ideal Client Experience: Imagine the experience you want each client to have and how your work contributes to their confidence and happiness. Focusing on the positive impact you make can be incredibly motivating.

• Keep a Journal of Client Feedback: Write down positive client feedback and moments that made you feel proud. Revisit these entries when you need a reminder of the difference you're making in people's lives.

Rediscovering your "why" connects you to the purpose behind your work, giving you the motivation to keep moving forward with passion and dedication.

Burnout Isn't the End—It's a Reminder to Realign

Burnout doesn't mean you're not cut out for this work; it's simply a reminder to realign, set boundaries, and prioritize what matters. When you approach burnout with a compassionate, proactive mindset, you're able to make adjustments that support both your well-being and your long-term success.

By protecting your energy, staying inspired, and embracing self-care, you're creating a career that's sustainable, fulfilling, and rich with purpose. Each day becomes an opportunity to grow, learn, and bring joy to the clients who trust you, reinforcing your dedication to excellence in every moment.

Adapting to Changing Trends and Client Expectations

Staying Relevant Without Losing Your Identity

In the beauty industry, trends come and go quickly, and clients often look to their stylist to keep them updated on what's new. Staying informed about trends is important, but there's a balance to strike. Adapting to changes doesn't mean shifting your entire style or trying to be everything to everyone—it's about selectively embracing what resonates with your brand and enhances the client experience.

When you're clear on your style, expertise, and brand values, it becomes easier to navigate trends with intention. You can choose the techniques and styles that align with your brand's identity, allowing you to stay relevant while remaining authentic. This approach not only strengthens your brand but also builds client trust, as they can rely on you to offer looks that feel both fresh and true to your expertise.

Choosing Trends that Add Value to Your Client Experience

Not every trend is worth adopting, and clients appreciate a stylist who provides expert guidance on what truly suits them. Choosing trends that add genuine value to your client experience helps you stay relevant while maintaining the quality and consistency clients expect.

- Prioritize Trends that Complement Your Specialty: Focus on trends that align with your area of expertise. If your brand is

196

built around precision cuts, for example, look for trends in cutting techniques or styles that bring fresh elements to your specialty.

- Consider Your Clients' Needs and Preferences: Think about your clients and what they value most. If a trend aligns with their lifestyle or aesthetic, it may be worth exploring. By choosing trends that resonate with your client base, you're reinforcing that you understand and care about their needs.

- Be Selective: Don't feel pressured to adopt every trend. Instead, filter out those that don't fit your brand, focusing on the ones that genuinely enhance your skill set and bring value to your clients. Your brand is defined as much by what you say "no" to as by what you embrace.

Being selective with trends allows you to curate a service menu that feels cohesive, thoughtful, and aligned with your unique vision.

Communicating Trends to Clients with Confidence

When a client requests a trendy style that may not suit them or doesn't align with your expertise, it's essential to communicate your perspective with confidence and empathy. Clients rely on you for guidance, and clear communication helps them feel understood and respected.

- Educate on Suitability: Explain why certain trends may or may not work for them based on factors like hair type, lifestyle, or face shape. Offer alternatives that capture the essence of the trend in a way that's more flattering or practical for them.

• Express Your Professional Insight: Share your honest opinion if a trend doesn't align with your expertise or their needs. For example, if a client wants a cut or color that you feel won't achieve the desired outcome, express this respectfully, emphasizing that your goal is always to create a look they'll love.

• Offer Compromise Solutions: When possible, find ways to adapt a trend to suit the client in a way that aligns with your skills. For instance, if a client wants an extreme color but prefers low maintenance, suggest a softer version that achieves a similar effect with less upkeep.

When clients feel that you have their best interests at heart, they're more likely to trust your recommendations and see you as an expert who prioritizes quality over novelty.

Building Flexibility into Your Brand

Flexibility doesn't mean compromising your brand—it means staying adaptable and open to change in a way that enhances your unique strengths. Building flexibility into your brand allows you to adjust with the industry while staying true to your core values.

• Set Aside Time for Exploration: Regularly explore new techniques, styles, or products to stay updated. Even if you don't adopt every trend, this practice keeps you informed, confident, and ready to discuss trends knowledgeably with clients.

• Incorporate Seasonal Updates: Refresh your service offerings seasonally with a few on-trend options. This shows clients that you're aware of what's current, while allowing you to focus on a limited selection that aligns with your brand.

•   Stay Open to Client Feedback: Listen to your clients' feedback and interests. If you notice a pattern in requests for certain styles or techniques, consider whether incorporating these trends could enhance your services without compromising your brand.

A flexible approach keeps your brand dynamic and responsive, showing clients that you're adaptable without diluting the essence of what makes you unique.

Balancing Trends with Timeless Expertise

While trends add excitement, your core expertise is what sets your brand apart. Balancing trendy elements with timeless skills creates a client experience that feels both current and enduring, reinforcing your position as a stylist who can deliver high-quality results regardless of trends.

•   Anchor Your Brand in Timeless Techniques: Continue to refine and showcase the skills you're known for, like precision cutting, color theory, or personalized consultations. These skills build a foundation of quality that clients trust.

•   Use Trends to Highlight Your Core Skills: For example, if a new texturizing technique aligns with your style, use it to enhance your existing services. This approach keeps your brand rooted in expertise while allowing you to bring fresh elements to your work.

- Communicate the Value of Quality: Remind clients that while trends are fun, quality and suitability are the foundation of any lasting look. This helps clients appreciate the value of timeless expertise, even when they're drawn to something trendy.

Balancing trends with timeless skills builds a brand that's adaptable, trustworthy, and always focused on delivering value to clients.

Trends Add Spice, but Expertise Builds Loyalty

Staying informed about trends keeps your work exciting, but it's your expertise, authenticity, and thoughtful approach that build lasting client loyalty. By being selective, adaptable, and clear in your communication, you're able to offer clients looks that feel fresh, personalized, and true to your brand.

In the end, trends may bring clients in, but it's your dedication to quality, honesty, and skill that keeps them coming back. Adapting to change without losing yourself allows you to create a brand that's both dynamic and grounded, ensuring that clients see you as a stylist who's not only relevant but also reliable, authentic, and focused on their unique needs.

Turning Setbacks into Learning Experiences

Why Setbacks are Part of the Journey

In any career, especially one as hands-on and dynamic as styling, setbacks are inevitable. Whether it's a service that didn't turn out as expected, a client who was difficult to satisfy, or a missed opportunity, setbacks are a natural part of growth. Instead of seeing these moments as failures, embracing them as learning experiences allows you to build resilience, improve your skills, and strengthen your brand.

Setbacks don't define your talent—they're just moments that reveal where there's room to grow. Each challenge teaches you something valuable, whether it's a skill to improve, a new approach to consider, or a mindset shift that helps you handle similar situations in the future. By approaching setbacks with curiosity instead of frustration, you're able to turn obstacles into stepping stones that move you closer to your goals.

Reflecting on Mistakes to Find Valuable Lessons

Every setback holds a lesson, but finding it requires reflection. Taking the time to look back on challenging moments allows you to gain insights, identify areas for improvement, and turn mistakes into growth opportunities.

- Break Down the Situation: Think through what

happened step-by-step. Identify where things went off track and any factors that may have contributed, such as time constraints, product choices, or communication gaps with the client. Breaking down the situation helps you see what was in your control and what was not.

• Acknowledge Your Emotions: It's natural to feel disappointed, frustrated, or even embarrassed by a setback. Allow yourself to process these emotions before diving into analysis. Acknowledging how you feel clears the way for a more objective, growth-focused perspective.

• Ask What You Would Do Differently: Consider what you would change if you were in the same situation again. This question allows you to identify practical steps for improvement, whether it's adjusting your approach, refining a technique, or enhancing communication with the client.

Reflecting on mistakes isn't about dwelling on what went wrong—it's about using each experience as a guide for future success, helping you approach similar challenges with confidence and clarity.

Using Client Feedback to Guide Improvement

Client feedback can be a powerful tool for growth, even when it's challenging to hear. Learning to accept and act on constructive feedback allows you to refine your skills and improve the client experience, making each service better than the last.

• Listen Without Defensiveness: When clients share feedback, listen openly, even if it's hard to hear. Try to see things from their perspective and focus on what you can learn from their experience.

- Ask Questions to Clarify: If a client's feedback feels vague or unclear, ask gentle questions to better understand their concerns. For example, "Could you share what you felt could have been different?" This approach shows clients that you value their perspective and are committed to improvement.

- Thank Clients for Their Honesty: Express gratitude to clients who take the time to provide feedback. Their input is valuable, and acknowledging it reinforces that you care about their satisfaction and are always striving to improve.

By treating feedback as a resource instead of a criticism, you're building a mindset that welcomes growth, strengthens client trust, and keeps you continuously refining your craft.

Turning Setbacks into Actionable Goals

One of the most effective ways to grow from setbacks is to set actionable goals that address the areas you want to improve. When you turn challenges into specific objectives, you're actively transforming obstacles into opportunities for growth.

- Identify Skills to Strengthen: If a setback revealed an area for improvement, set a goal to build that skill. For example, if a client was unhappy with a color treatment, consider enrolling in an advanced color workshop to deepen your expertise.

- Practice Specific Techniques: Set a goal to practice

203

specific techniques regularly. Consistent practice allows you to gain confidence, perfect your skills, and feel prepared for similar situations in the future.

• Develop New Communication Strategies: If communication was a factor in the setback, set goals around improving your consultation or listening skills. Clear communication is essential for client satisfaction, and refining this skill can prevent misunderstandings and ensure each client feels heard.

By turning setbacks into actionable goals, you're using each challenge as a catalyst for improvement, transforming frustration into forward momentum.

Cultivating a Growth Mindset

A growth mindset is the belief that abilities and intelligence can be developed through effort and learning. When you approach setbacks with a growth mindset, you're better able to embrace challenges, learn from mistakes, and continually improve.

• Reframe Challenges as Opportunities: When you encounter a setback, remind yourself that it's a chance to grow, not a reflection of your abilities. This mindset shift allows you to stay focused on progress, even in difficult moments.

• Celebrate Small Wins: Growth isn't always about big leaps—it's often a series of small, consistent improvements. Acknowledge and celebrate each step forward, no matter how minor it may seem.

•　　　Stay Open to Learning: Embrace every opportunity to learn, whether it's from feedback, a workshop, or a challenging client. A growth mindset keeps you open to new ideas and ready to adapt, building a career that's resilient and constantly evolving.

When you view each setback as a learning experience, you're building a mindset that's focused on growth, improvement, and long-term success.

Strengthening Your Brand Through Resilience

Resilience is a quality that clients notice and value. When clients see that you handle setbacks with grace, openness, and a commitment to improvement, it reinforces their trust in your expertise and professionalism. Resilience shows clients that you're dedicated to delivering quality, even in the face of challenges.

•　　　Share Your Growth Journey: When appropriate, let clients know about the steps you're taking to improve. For example, if you've completed a course or practiced a technique based on client feedback, mention it in conversation or on social media. This transparency reinforces that you're always working to provide the best.

•　　　Show Gratitude for Client Patience: If a client was part of a challenging experience, thank them for their patience and understanding. Acknowledging their support strengthens your relationship and shows that you value their role in your journey.

•　　　Demonstrate Consistency and Improvement: Show

clients that you're consistently working to enhance their experience. Over time, your commitment to growth will strengthen their loyalty and make them proud to be part of your brand's evolution.

Resilience isn't just about handling setbacks—it's about using each challenge to build a stronger, more trustworthy brand that clients respect and admire.

Setbacks Are Steps Forward

In the end, setbacks are not barriers—they're stepping stones that push you to refine your skills, expand your perspective, and build a career that's both dynamic and resilient. Each challenge you face and overcome becomes part of the foundation that makes your brand unique, trustworthy, and capable of lasting success.

By embracing setbacks as opportunities for growth, you're not only improving your skills but also cultivating a mindset that's focused on progress, learning, and continual improvement. This resilience builds a brand that clients recognize, respect, and trust, setting you apart as a stylist who's dedicated to excellence, no matter the challenges along the way.

Exercise: Building Your Resilience Toolkit

Step 1: Identify Common Challenges

Start by identifying the types of challenges you encounter most frequently in your work. Recognizing these common obstacles helps you prepare, so they feel manageable instead of overwhelming when they arise.

- List Your Top Challenges: Think about the challenges you've faced, whether it's difficult client requests, service outcomes that didn't meet expectations, or periods of low energy. Write down 3-5 common challenges you encounter.
- Reflect on How They Affect You: Note how each challenge typically impacts you, both emotionally and professionally. For example, do you feel anxious, frustrated, or discouraged? Understanding these reactions allows you to develop strategies that address both the practical and emotional aspects.

Knowing your top challenges is the first step in building a resilience toolkit that's tailored to your unique experiences.

Step 2: Create Strategies for Each Challenge

For each challenge you've listed, brainstorm strategies that help you navigate or overcome it. These strategies can be practical steps, mindset shifts, or actions that build resilience and reduce stress.

• Choose Practical Solutions: If a challenge involves a skill or technical area, consider resources like workshops, practice sessions, or expert guidance to improve your approach. For example, if color corrections are challenging, a refresher course could increase your confidence.

• Develop Mindset Shifts: For challenges that affect your emotions or mindset, write down positive reminders or affirmations. For instance, if you feel anxious about client feedback, remind yourself that constructive feedback is part of growth and not a reflection of your worth.

• Plan Actions to Reduce Stress: Identify actions that help you stay calm and centered. This could include deep breathing, a quick walk, or taking a moment to refocus before addressing the challenge. Small, intentional actions can make a big difference in how you handle stress.

Creating a strategy for each challenge turns your resilience toolkit into a practical resource you can rely on when obstacles arise.

Step 3: Set Up a Support System

Resilience isn't something you have to build alone. A support system of peers, mentors, or friends who understand your journey can provide valuable perspective, encouragement, and advice.

• Identify Key People in Your Network: Write down 2-3 people you can turn to for support. This might be a mentor, a stylist friend, or a family member who listens without judgment. These people can provide guidance and remind you that you're not alone.

•   Create a Plan for Reaching Out: Decide how you'll connect with your support system when needed. Whether it's a quick text, a coffee chat, or a phone call, having a plan in place makes it easier to seek support when challenges arise.

A strong support system enhances your resilience, giving you the confidence to face obstacles knowing you have people who believe in you.

Step 4: Practice Self-Compassion

Self-compassion is key to resilience, helping you handle setbacks without being overly critical. Practicing self-compassion means treating yourself with kindness and understanding, especially when things don't go as planned.

•   Write a Compassionate Affirmation: Choose a phrase or affirmation that reminds you to be gentle with yourself, like "I'm allowed to make mistakes as part of my growth journey" or "Every challenge is an opportunity to learn." Repeat this affirmation whenever you need a reminder to stay compassionate.

•   Acknowledge Your Progress: Regularly take time to reflect on your achievements, both big and small. Celebrating progress reinforces that you're growing and making strides, even when challenges arise.

Self-compassion makes it easier to bounce back from setbacks, empowering you to move forward without self-doubt.

Your Resilience Toolkit: A Resource for Growth

With your resilience toolkit in place, you're equipped to handle challenges with confidence and perspective. Each strategy, support system, and affirmation reinforces your ability to navigate obstacles, turning setbacks into opportunities for growth. By building resilience, you're creating a career that's adaptable, fulfilling, and rich with learning moments that bring you closer to your goals.

Your toolkit isn't just a response to challenges—it's a resource that empowers you to grow, learn, and build a brand that's both resilient and inspiring.

Wrap-Up and Next Steps

Summary of Key Takeaways

In this chapter, you've built a framework for navigating challenges with resilience, seeing each obstacle as an opportunity for growth. From preventing burnout and staying inspired to adapting to trends while staying true to your brand, you now have tools to overcome setbacks in a way that strengthens both your skills and client relationships.

You've learned the value of reflecting on mistakes, using client feedback to guide improvement, and building a resilience toolkit that prepares you for the unexpected. By embracing each challenge with a growth-oriented mindset, you're building a career that's adaptable, grounded, and ready to thrive, no matter what comes your way.

Next Steps

With resilience as a foundation, it's time to look beyond the immediate challenges and focus on the lasting impact you want to create. In the next chapter, we'll explore Beyond the Chair: Building a Career that Impacts and Inspires. You'll learn strategies to expand your influence, create meaningful connections with clients, and develop a legacy that goes beyond individual appointments.

Get ready to explore how your work can create lasting value, impacting clients and the industry in ways that resonate on a deeper level.

CHAPTER NINE: BEYOND THE CHAIR—BUILDING A CAREER THAT IMPACTS AND INSPIRES

Building a career that transcends the chair requires purpose, faith, and a commitment to serving others. My friend Keijuane exemplifies this in every way. His unwavering grit, radiant smile, and deep-rooted faith create a ripple effect in the community, touching lives and inspiring transformation. Watching him connect with others and lead with purpose has taught me the power of aligning my work with something greater than myself.

Keijuane's example has shown me that creating impact isn't solely about skill or effort; it's about believing in a higher purpose and trusting in the greater orchestration of life. To truly fulfill my calling, I've realized I must lead with my heart, stay grounded in faith, and remain spiritually connected. This alignment fuels not only my work behind the chair but also my dedication to teaching, volunteering, and creating resources that empower others.

By plugging into this sense of purpose and faith, I've discovered that my career isn't just about hair—it's about inspiring transformation, uplifting my community, and leaving a legacy. It's this connection that propels me beyond the chair and into a life of meaningful impact and inspiration.

Why Creating Impact Matters

Your Work is More Than Just a Service

In the beauty industry, it's easy to focus solely on the technical side of styling—perfecting cuts, mastering color, and meeting clients' aesthetic goals. But when you approach your work with the intention of creating impact, it becomes more than just a service. You're not just enhancing appearances; you're building confidence, supporting self-expression, and inspiring clients to see themselves in a new light.

Creating impact means seeing every client interaction as a chance to leave a lasting impression. It's about the conversations, the kindness, and the genuine connections that transform your services into something meaningful. When clients feel understood, valued, and empowered by their experience with you, they're more than satisfied—they're truly moved, and they remember that feeling.

How Impact Enhances Client Loyalty and Fulfillment

When your work goes beyond a service, it naturally fosters client loyalty. Clients want more than a great cut or color; they want an experience that feels personal and positive, one that enriches their lives beyond the chair. By prioritizing connection, you're creating a brand that clients feel loyal to, one they turn to for both style and support.

The impact you create also brings fulfillment to your own journey.

213

Knowing that your work has a positive effect on others, that you're helping clients feel seen and appreciated, adds depth and purpose to your career. This sense of fulfillment is what turns a job into a calling, motivating you to keep growing, learning, and refining your craft.

Building a Brand with Lasting Influence

A career that impacts and inspires doesn't happen by accident—it's built intentionally, with each client interaction, each small act of kindness, and each choice to go above and beyond. When you commit to creating impact, you're shaping a brand that's known for quality, care, and authenticity. Clients see you not just as a stylist but as a trusted figure who enhances their lives, helping them feel more confident, empowered, and valued.

In the end, creating impact is about the legacy you're building. It's about how your work affects others and what you'll be remembered for. By focusing on impact, you're creating a career that goes beyond appointments, becoming a source of strength, inspiration, and support in your clients' lives.

Building Deep Connections with Clients

The Power of Genuine Connection

Building a genuine connection with clients is about more than just delivering a great service—it's about making them feel seen, heard, and valued. When clients sit in your chair, they're looking for more than just a new style; they're looking for an experience that feels personal. Each appointment is a chance to create a moment of trust and connection, showing clients that you're not only invested in their appearance but in their confidence and comfort as well.

A deep connection is what transforms an appointment from a routine service into a meaningful experience. Clients remember the stylist who listens, who takes the time to understand what they want, and who makes them feel cared for. These are the interactions that keep clients coming back, building loyalty that goes beyond just liking the result—they're loyal to the way you make them feel.

Active Listening as the Foundation of Connection

One of the most powerful ways to build a connection is through active listening. When clients feel that you're truly listening, they feel understood, and that understanding is the foundation of trust.

- Start with Open-Ended Questions: Encourage clients to share their thoughts, not just about their hair but about their goals, concerns, or any recent changes they're experiencing. Simple questions like, "What are you hoping to achieve with your style today?" or "What's working and what isn't?" create a conversation that goes beyond surface-level preferences.
- Listen with Curiosity and Empathy: When clients share their thoughts, listen without jumping in or interrupting. Make eye contact, nod, and give them space to express themselves fully. This approach shows that you value their input and are committed to

creating a result that aligns with their vision.

•   Reflect and Confirm: Once a client has shared their preferences or concerns, repeat back what you've heard in your own words. For example, "It sounds like you're looking for something low-maintenance but still polished. Does that feel right?" Reflecting back reinforces that you've understood and respects the client's vision.

Active listening isn't just a skill; it's a way of showing clients that they matter, building trust and setting the tone for a meaningful connection.

Creating a Comfortable and Welcoming Space

Clients remember how they feel when they're with you, and creating a welcoming environment is key to establishing trust. A comfortable space lets clients relax and opens the door to deeper, more personal conversations.

•   Set a Positive, Relaxing Tone: Small details like soft music, a pleasant fragrance, or a comfortable chair can make a big difference. These elements create a warm atmosphere that puts clients at ease from the moment they walk in.

•   Show Genuine Interest: Simple gestures like asking about their day or remembering small details from previous conversations show that you care about them as individuals. These small acts of kindness make clients feel valued and appreciated.

•   Respect Their Energy: Not every client wants a deep conversation. Some may need a quiet, relaxing appointment. Reading their cues and respecting their energy shows clients that you're tuned in to their needs, whether they're looking for a chat or a peaceful break.

A comfortable, welcoming environment reinforces that you're there to make their experience as enjoyable and tailored as possible, building a foundation of respect and trust.

Personalizing Each Client's Experience

Personalization is what makes every client feel unique. When you tailor the experience to their specific needs and preferences, you're showing that you see them as individuals, not just another appointment on the schedule.

- Remember Personal Details: Keep notes on clients' preferences, past styles, or any special occasions they mention. Bringing these details up in conversation, like remembering a client's preferred styling products or asking about their recent vacation, shows that you're genuinely engaged.
- Adjust Based on Feedback: After a service, ask clients if there's anything they'd like to adjust. Listening to their feedback and being open to small changes builds confidence that you're focused on their satisfaction above all else.
- Create Rituals for Regulars: For clients who return regularly, establish small rituals that make their experience memorable, like a preferred drink, a favorite magazine, or a styling

tip specific to their needs. These personal touches set you apart and deepen the sense of loyalty.

When clients see that you remember the little things, it reinforces that you value them, creating an experience that feels custom-made every time.

How Meaningful Connections Build Loyalty

Loyalty doesn't just come from delivering a beautiful end result—it comes from the way you make clients feel. When clients know that you genuinely care about them, they're not just clients—they're part of a trusted community. They know that they're valued, respected, and welcomed in your space, and that loyalty extends beyond any single appointment.

Each connection you build strengthens your brand, creating a reputation for care, professionalism, and authenticity. Clients who feel valued are more likely to return, refer friends, and trust you with new styles or ideas. These meaningful relationships are the heart of your brand, making your work fulfilling and impactful.

In the end, deep connections are what set your brand apart. By going beyond the service, listening actively, creating comfort, and personalizing each experience, you're building a career that's more than just about styling—it's about making a difference in each client's life.

Becoming a Source of Inspiration in Your Community

Why Community Involvement Matters

Your brand isn't just built within the walls of your salon—it extends into your community, reaching people who may not even be clients. By sharing your expertise, supporting local events, or simply being a positive influence, you're establishing a presence that reflects your values and connects with people on a deeper level.

When you engage with your community, you're not only giving back but also creating opportunities to inspire, educate, and connect. People are drawn to stylists who are actively involved, who use their skills and voice to uplift others. This sense of connection strengthens your brand, as people begin to see you not just as a professional, but as a figure who genuinely cares about their community.

Sharing Your Knowledge and Passion

One of the most powerful ways to inspire others is by sharing your knowledge. Your skills and insights have the potential to educate, support, and even spark interest in those looking to learn more about hair, beauty, or self-care.

•	Host Local Workshops: Offer workshops that teach basic styling techniques, hair care tips, or DIY maintenance. These events give people a chance to interact with you, learn something valuable, and experience your expertise firsthand. Workshops can be tailored to different groups, like teens, parents, or professionals, making them inclusive and accessible.

• Offer Free Consultations at Community Events: Many local events welcome professionals to provide free mini-consultations. Use these opportunities to connect with new faces, share personalized advice, and showcase your brand's dedication to helping people feel confident.

• Collaborate with Local Businesses: Partner with nearby businesses, such as fitness studios, boutiques, or wellness centers, to host joint events. This cross-promotion helps you reach a wider audience and demonstrates your commitment to building a supportive community.

By sharing your knowledge, you're positioning yourself as an approachable expert, someone people can trust for guidance and inspiration.

Supporting Causes that Reflect Your Values

Aligning your brand with causes that matter to you not only amplifies your impact but also reinforces your authenticity. Clients and community members appreciate seeing stylists who use their platform to support meaningful initiatives, whether it's raising awareness for mental health, supporting small businesses, or championing eco-friendly practices.

• Participate in Charity Events: Look for local charity events that align with your values. Whether it's styling for a fundraiser, donating a portion of proceeds, or volunteering your time, these efforts show your community that you're invested in more than just business.

• Organize Your Own Initiatives: If there's a cause you're passionate about, consider organizing a small event to raise funds or awareness. For example, you could host a donation-based event where proceeds go to a local shelter or environmental organization. Leading these initiatives allows you to create a positive impact that's closely aligned with your values.

• Use Your Platform for Awareness: Social media offers a space to share messages that reflect your beliefs. Use your online presence to highlight causes you care about, share educational posts, or promote awareness on topics that resonate with you and your brand.

Supporting causes that reflect your values isn't just about charity— it's about showing that your brand has heart, purpose, and a commitment to making a difference.

Becoming a Mentor and Role Model

Your experience, insight, and skills are valuable resources, especially for newcomers in the industry. By mentoring, you're not only contributing to the growth of others but also enriching your own journey as you share your knowledge, reflect on your path, and build meaningful relationships.

• Offer Mentorship to New Stylists: Reach out to

beauty schools, training programs, or salons looking for mentors. Your guidance can help shape the next generation of stylists, supporting them through challenges and encouraging them to find their own voice in the industry.

•   Create an Online Community: If local mentorship isn't possible, consider building an online community where you can offer advice, answer questions, and provide support. This could be through social media groups, webinars, or online Q&A sessions, allowing you to connect with aspiring stylists no matter where they are.

•   Be Transparent About Your Journey: Share the challenges, triumphs, and lessons you've learned. This honesty makes you relatable and inspires others who may be facing similar challenges. When people see that you've navigated obstacles and grown stronger, they're encouraged to pursue their own path with resilience.

Being a mentor and role model allows you to extend your impact beyond clients, leaving a lasting impression on those who look up to you for guidance and inspiration.

Creating a Lasting Presence in Your Community

A strong presence in your community is built over time, with consistent, genuine interactions that show people who you are and what you stand for. By actively engaging, you're reinforcing your brand as one that's dedicated to supporting, inspiring, and connecting with others.

• Make Community Involvement a Regular Practice: Set aside time each month or quarter to participate in community events, host workshops, or volunteer. Consistency reinforces that your brand is genuinely invested in the community.

• Show Appreciation to Your Community: Share messages of gratitude on social media or through newsletters, thanking your clients and community for their support. Small gestures like this show that you value their role in your journey and that you see them as part of your brand's story.

• Celebrate Community Achievements: Use your platform to recognize milestones, events, or local successes. Celebrating others' achievements creates a culture of positivity and support that people associate with your brand.

When people see your commitment to the community, they understand that your brand goes beyond business. You're not just providing a service—you're building relationships, supporting causes, and creating a network of people who value and respect what you bring to the table.

Leaving a Legacy That Reflects Your Values

What Does Legacy Mean to You?

A legacy isn't just about the work you do today—it's about the lasting impression you leave behind. Your legacy is the culmination of your values, the impact you make, and the ways people remember your influence long after an appointment. For some, a legacy may mean being known as a stylist who brought out the best in every client. For others, it might be about inspiring confidence, supporting others in the industry, or simply making a positive difference.

Defining what legacy means to you gives purpose to your journey, guiding the choices you make and shaping the way you approach each client, event, and community interaction. When you're clear on the legacy you want to create, every action aligns with that vision, building a brand that resonates deeply and leaves a lasting impact.

Defining the Values You Want to Be Known For

Values are the foundation of your legacy—they're the principles that guide your decisions, interactions, and overall approach. Whether it's a commitment to quality, a focus on empowering clients, or a dedication to continuous learning, defining your values helps you establish a clear direction for your brand.

- Identify Your Core Values: Take time to reflect on what matters most to you in your work. These might include qualities like authenticity, creativity, respect, or compassion. Write down 3-5 values that resonate deeply and feel aligned with your vision.
- Consider the Impact of Each Value: Think about how each value shows up in your day-to-day work and how it affects your clients. For example, if authenticity is a core value, consider how it influences your communication style, client relationships, and the way you approach styling.

• Commit to Living These Values: A legacy is built through consistency, so commit to embodying these values in every interaction. When clients see that your actions consistently reflect your values, they understand what you stand for and trust the authenticity of your brand.

By defining and embodying your values, you're creating a foundation for a legacy that feels meaningful, intentional, and true to who you are.

Setting Goals for a Lasting Impact

Once you're clear on your values, it's time to set specific goals that support the legacy you want to create. These goals serve as milestones on your journey, helping you make choices that align with your vision for impact.

• Identify Long-Term Goals: Think about the lasting difference you want to make in the industry, for your clients, or within your community. Long-term goals might include things like mentoring new stylists, creating a signature course, or supporting a cause that matters to you.

• Break Down Goals into Achievable Steps: Legacy-building goals can feel big, but breaking them down makes them manageable. For example, if your goal is to mentor others, start by setting up informational sessions, reaching out to beauty schools, or offering virtual advice sessions.

• Evaluate and Adjust: Legacy isn't static—it evolves

with you. Regularly revisit your goals and values to ensure they still resonate with your vision. Adjust as needed to stay aligned with the impact you want to create.

Setting intentional goals keeps you focused on the bigger picture, allowing each step to contribute to a legacy that's authentic and lasting.

Leaving a Positive Impact on Each Client

Every client interaction is an opportunity to reinforce your legacy. When you approach each appointment with the goal of leaving a positive impact, you're building relationships that clients remember long after they leave your chair.

- Focus on Confidence and Empowerment: Beyond the haircut or color, think about how you can make each client feel confident, empowered, and uplifted. Small gestures, like a compliment or personalized advice, reinforce that you care about their overall well-being.
- Provide Lasting Education: Share tips and insights that clients can use to maintain their look at home. Educating clients shows that you're invested in their experience beyond the appointment, leaving them with tools that add value to their routine.
- Follow Up for Continued Connection: After a major style change or new treatment, consider reaching out to check in. A simple follow-up shows that you're invested in their satisfaction, reinforcing the personal connection and leaving a positive impression.

When clients see that you're dedicated to their happiness and confidence, they're more likely to view you as a trusted partner in their self-expression, strengthening the foundation of your legacy.

Inspiring Others Through Your Work

A powerful legacy doesn't just impact clients—it also inspires others in the industry. By sharing your journey, supporting newcomers, and being open about your experiences, you're creating a positive influence that extends beyond your own work.

- Share Your Knowledge Generously: Whether it's through social media, blog posts, or workshops, sharing what you've learned creates a ripple effect. Stylists who feel encouraged and inspired by your work will carry that influence forward, amplifying your impact.
- Encourage Authenticity in Others: Inspire other stylists to embrace their unique style and voice. When they see you thriving by staying true to yourself, they're encouraged to pursue their own path with confidence.
- Be Transparent About Challenges: Sharing the ups and downs of your journey makes you relatable and reminds others that setbacks are a natural part of growth. By being open about your challenges, you're creating a culture of resilience and authenticity that inspires others to keep going.

Inspiring others through your work adds depth to your legacy, creating a network of professionals who share your values and carry forward your influence.

Creating a Lasting Presence in Your Community

A legacy extends beyond individual interactions, shaping the community that surrounds you. Being a positive influence within your community not only strengthens your brand but also contributes to a culture of support, kindness, and inspiration.

- Engage in Community Initiatives Regularly: Set aside time each year to participate in community events or support local causes. Consistency reinforces your presence, showing the community that your involvement is genuine and lasting.
- Highlight Local Successes: Use your platform to celebrate others in your community, whether it's other small businesses, local talent, or charitable initiatives. Supporting and uplifting others enriches your community and positions your brand as a source of positivity.
- Encourage a Culture of Giving Back: By showing your commitment to giving back, you're setting an example that encourages others to do the same. This creates a community where kindness, generosity, and support are values that everyone upholds.

A lasting presence in your community is about creating positive change, leaving an impact that resonates with everyone who encounters your brand.

Building a Legacy That Reflects Who You Are

Legacy isn't built in a day—it's the result of consistent, intentional choices that reflect who you are and what you stand for. By defining your values, setting purposeful goals, and creating a positive impact on clients, peers, and your community, you're building a career that's more than just work. You're leaving a lasting imprint that will be remembered long after.

In the end, a legacy is about how you make people feel, the influence you share, and the values you represent. It's the trust, respect, and inspiration you cultivate, creating a career that goes beyond appointments, trends, or techniques. By building a legacy that reflects your values, you're creating a brand that inspires, uplifts, and impacts others in meaningful ways—one that's truly unforgettable.

Exercise: Crafting Your Impact Statement

Step 1: Reflect on Your Core Values

Begin by identifying the values that are most important to you in your work. Think about what truly motivates you, what you want clients to feel, and the principles that guide your decisions. This step is about grounding yourself in the qualities you want to represent.

- Write Down Your Key Values: Consider values like authenticity, compassion, confidence-building, or continuous growth.

Choose 3-5 values that resonate deeply with your vision for your brand.

- Describe Each Value's Purpose: For each value, write a brief sentence about why it matters to you. For example, "Compassion allows me to connect with clients on a deeper level, helping them feel valued and understood."

By reflecting on your core values, you're establishing the foundation of your impact statement, ensuring it feels personal, authentic, and meaningful.

Step 2: Identify the Lasting Impact You Want to Create

Next, think about the impression you want to leave with clients, peers, and your community. Consider the influence you hope to have, not only in your services but in the confidence, trust, and inspiration you give others.

- Define Your Impact on Clients: Think about how you want clients to feel after each appointment. Perhaps you want them to feel confident, empowered, or uplifted. Describe this impact in a few words.
- Consider Your Influence on the Industry: Reflect on how you want to inspire others in the beauty industry. This could include promoting authenticity, encouraging continuous learning, or supporting new stylists. Write a sentence about the influence you hope to have.
- Outline Your Contribution to the Community: Think

about how you want to engage with and support your community. This could be through service, mentorship, or advocacy for causes you believe in. Summarize your desired community impact.

These descriptions will shape the vision of your legacy, giving purpose to the actions you take and the connections you build.

Step 3: Bring It All Together

Now, combine your values and desired impact into a concise statement that captures the essence of your legacy. Your impact statement should reflect who you are, what you stand for, and the lasting difference you want to make.

- Create a Draft: Start with a phrase like, "My mission is to…" or "I'm committed to…" followed by your core values and the impact you want to create. For example, "My mission is to empower clients through authentic, compassionate service, inspiring confidence in each person I work with, while uplifting my community through support and education."
- Refine for Clarity and Authenticity: Read your draft aloud and make adjustments until it feels natural and true to your voice. Aim for a statement that's concise but powerful, capturing the heart of what you want your legacy to be.

Your impact statement should feel like a clear, honest reflection of the legacy you're building, one that you can return to for inspiration and guidance.

Step 4: Integrate Your Impact Statement into Your Daily Work

Your impact statement isn't just a phrase to look back on—it's a living reminder of the purpose behind everything you do. Find ways to integrate it into your daily work to keep your goals and values at the forefront.

- Display It in Your Workspace: Keep a copy of your impact statement in your salon, studio, or workspace. Seeing it regularly will remind you of the values you're committed to upholding.
- Share It with Clients and Peers: Consider sharing your impact statement on your website, social media, or in conversations with clients. When people know what you stand for, they connect with your brand on a deeper level.
- Reflect on It Regularly: At the end of each week or month, reflect on how you've aligned with your impact statement. This practice helps you stay centered on your goals and make adjustments as needed.

Your impact statement serves as a guiding light, helping you stay true to the legacy you want to create, inspiring you to show up each day with purpose, authenticity, and confidence.

Your Impact Statement: A Vision for Legacy

With your impact statement in place, you've defined the legacy you want to build—a brand that goes beyond beauty to inspire, empower, and connect. This statement isn't just a goal; it's a reflection of the passion and values you bring to your work. Each day, as you connect with clients, engage with your community, and refine your skills, you're living this vision, creating a career that truly makes a difference.

Wrap-Up and Next Steps

Summary of Key Takeaways

In this chapter, you've explored what it means to create a career that impacts and inspires. From building deep connections with clients and becoming a source of support in your community to defining a legacy that reflects your values, each action you take contributes to a brand that's memorable, respected, and genuine.

By crafting your impact statement, you've outlined the vision and purpose behind your work—a guiding reminder of the positive difference you aim to make every day. This legacy isn't just about what you do; it's about the way you make people feel, the values you uphold, and the confidence you inspire in others. When you focus on impact, your work transcends individual appointments, creating a career that's deeply rewarding for you and the clients you serve.

Next Steps

With a solid foundation for lasting impact, we'll now turn to the financial side of building a fulfilling career. In the final chapter, Living Financial Freedom: Breaking Free from the Need for Variety and Focusing on Wealth, you'll learn strategies to achieve long-term financial security, maintain wealth, and ensure that your passion translates into a sustainable, profitable career.

Get ready to explore how focus, mastery, and smart financial planning can lead you to a career that's not only impactful but also financially free.

Chapter Ten: Living Financial Freedom— Breaking Free from the Need for Variety and Focusing on Wealth

There came a moment when I realized my journey was no longer about what I lacked, but about embracing change. The more I committed to my own transformation, the more abundance started flowing into my life. I began to understand that true wealth isn't just about financial gain; it's about the becoming process—the growth, the wisdom, the strength that builds over time. That's where wealth really lives.

I'd spend time sitting with my sense of lack in meditation, examining it and challenging it. Instead of letting scarcity control me, I allowed myself to explore it and learn from it. Each meditation reminded me that lack is temporary and change is constant. The more I focused on what I was becoming, rather than what I didn't have, the more I saw my business and life start to flourish.

This shift led me to develop a wealth mindset. I no longer saw my work as just a skill; I saw it as a path to creating something that would support me even beyond the salon chair. I invested in resources, built a brand around my specialty, and began to see wealth not as something I chased, but as something I attracted through consistent growth and self-investment.

Redefining Success: Focusing on Wealth over Variety

There came a moment when I realized my journey was no longer about what I lacked, but about embracing change. The more I committed to my own transformation, the more abundance started flowing into my life. I began to understand that true wealth isn't just about financial gain; it's about the becoming process—the growth, the wisdom, the strength that builds over time. That's where wealth really lives.

I'd spend time sitting with my sense of lack in meditation, examining it and challenging it. Instead of letting scarcity control me, I allowed myself to explore it and learn from it. Each meditation reminded me that lack is temporary and change is constant. The more I focused on what I was becoming, rather than what I didn't have, the more I saw my business and life start to flourish.

This shift led me to develop something I call a wealth mindset. I no longer saw my work as just a skill; I saw it as a path to creating something that would support me even beyond the salon chair. I invested in resources, built a brand around my specialty, and began to see wealth not as something I chased, but as something I attract through consistent growth and self-investment.

Why Specialization is the Key to Financial Freedom

In an industry where variety is often celebrated, it can feel counterintuitive to focus on one area. But success doesn't always come from doing more—it comes from doing what you do best, with absolute mastery. Specialization is about honing in on a niche, becoming known for one thing you do exceptionally well, and building a reputation that clients trust. When you become a true expert in your niche, you're able to attract clients who value your unique skill, allowing you to charge premium rates and build a consistent, loyal clientele.

The path to financial freedom isn't paved by constantly adding more services. Instead, it's about building a brand that's laser-focused, confident, and recognized for excellence in one area. This approach doesn't just elevate your work—it gives you the stability, income, and freedom to shape your career on your terms.

How Focus Leads to Greater Stability and Income

When you commit to a specific focus, you're creating a foundation of consistency in both client satisfaction and income. Specialization attracts clients who are willing to pay more for an expert, knowing they'll receive a high-quality, tailored experience. Each appointment becomes more than a transaction; it's an investment in your reputation, and clients value that.

- Develop a Recognizable Brand: When you specialize,

your brand becomes synonymous with excellence in your niche. Clients remember you for the unique service you provide, making you the go-to stylist in that area.

•   Attract Premium Clients: Clients seeking a specialist are often willing to invest in quality. This allows you to raise your rates without losing clients, as your reputation and expertise justify the premium pricing.

•   Achieve Consistent Income: A specialized service creates a steady demand, as clients who value your expertise return regularly. This consistency ensures a reliable income stream, reducing the stress of constantly seeking new clients.

By narrowing your focus, you're building a career that's both financially rewarding and secure, giving you the freedom to grow without the pressure of constantly diversifying.

Embracing Simplicity for Greater Impact

Sometimes, the simplest path is the most powerful. By choosing to master one area and make it exceptional, you're creating a brand that resonates with clients who value quality over variety. They come to you because they know you deliver results that reflect years of dedication, skill, and focus.

Financial freedom isn't about having a wide range of services—it's about creating a service so impactful that clients will keep coming back. When you focus on wealth over variety, you're not just simplifying your career—you're building a legacy of quality, expertise, and stability.

The Power of Focused Mastery

Why Mastery Matters More Than Variety

In a world that often pushes the idea of doing more, there's something powerful about mastering one thing exceptionally well. When you choose to focus on a specific niche, you're building a foundation of trust, reliability, and quality that clients recognize and value. Mastery isn't just about skill—it's about becoming the stylist clients turn to for something they know only you can deliver.

Focused mastery allows you to charge higher rates because clients understand the depth of expertise behind each service. They're not just paying for a haircut or style; they're investing in a refined skill, honed through practice, dedication, and a commitment to excellence. This approach builds not only financial stability but also client loyalty, as clients know they can depend on you for consistent, high-quality results.

Steps to Ensure Financial Rewards from Your Expertise

Mastering a niche doesn't just happen by accident—it's a purposeful commitment to developing your skills and refining your techniques to an expert level. Here's how to ensure that your expertise translates into financial rewards:

• Invest in Continued Education: To stay at the top of your niche, commit to ongoing learning. Attend workshops, take advanced courses, and seek mentorship opportunities that deepen your skills. This dedication to growth shows clients that you're always evolving, ensuring they receive the best.

• Create a Signature Service: Develop a service that reflects your unique approach and expertise. This could be a specific type of cut, a custom color technique, or a unique styling method. A signature service differentiates you from other stylists, making you the go-to for that specialty.

• Refine Your Client Experience: Mastery isn't just about technique; it's about delivering a memorable experience. From personalized consultations to the ambiance you create, make every interaction intentional and focused on quality. Clients who feel valued and cared for are more likely to pay premium rates and return for the experience.

By refining your craft and focusing on excellence, you're creating a brand that clients trust and are willing to invest in, knowing they're receiving a service they can't find elsewhere.

Charging Premium Rates as an Expert

Clients recognize the value of expertise, and they're willing to pay for it. By positioning yourself as a specialist, you're able to command higher rates because clients understand the level of skill, care, and precision that goes into each service. They're not just looking for a cut or color—they're looking for an expert.

• Know Your Worth: Understand the value of your expertise, and don't hesitate to price your services accordingly. When you've invested time, energy, and resources into perfecting your skill, your rates should reflect that dedication.

• Communicate the Value of Your Service: Help clients understand what sets your service apart, whether it's the precision, the customization, or the lasting quality. Clients are more likely to invest when they feel educated on the unique value they're receiving.

• Maintain Consistent Quality: Premium pricing comes with an expectation of consistent quality. Ensure that every client receives the same level of care and expertise, building trust and reinforcing that your rates reflect an exceptional, reliable experience.

Charging premium rates isn't just about making more money—it's about aligning your pricing with the value you bring, allowing you to work with clients who respect and appreciate your skill.

Mastery Builds Client Loyalty and Stability

When clients see that you're a true master in your niche, they become loyal to your brand, trusting that you'll consistently deliver the quality and expertise they value. This loyalty creates a stable client base, ensuring that you're not constantly searching for new clients but instead nurturing relationships with those who return time and again.

• Build Relationships with Regulars: Invest in the clients who appreciate your expertise. Offer small, personalized touches that make their experience memorable, whether it's a tailored tip for maintenance or a follow-up message after a new style. These gestures reinforce the bond and make clients feel valued.

• Encourage Referrals: Satisfied clients who value your expertise are more likely to refer friends and family. Encourage referrals by letting clients know you appreciate word-of-mouth support, perhaps offering a small incentive for each referral.

• Establish Yourself as an Authority: Share insights, tips, or behind-the-scenes content that reflects your expertise. When clients see you as a thought leader in your niche, it builds trust and reinforces that they've chosen the right stylist.

Client loyalty isn't built on variety—it's built on trust, consistency, and a dedication to excellence that clients know they can count on.

Focused Mastery Leads to Financial Freedom

By choosing to focus on mastery, you're not just creating a niche—you're creating a brand that clients feel proud to support, one that stands out for its quality and reliability. Mastery allows you to build a career where you're financially secure, respected, and free from the pressures of constantly diversifying. You're working smarter, not harder, building wealth by delivering unparalleled value in one area that you excel in.

When you focus on what you do best, you're creating a career that's not only financially rewarding but deeply fulfilling. Each appointment reinforces your brand, your skills, and the trust clients have in you, leading to a career that's both impactful and financially free.

Building a System for Financial Growth

The Importance of Financial Organization

Achieving financial freedom isn't just about charging premium rates—it's about creating a system that keeps your income steady, tracks your progress, and allows you to make informed financial decisions. Financial organization gives you a clear picture of where your money is coming from, where it's going, and how it's growing. This system ensures that you're not just earning well but building wealth that supports your long-term vision.

Having a solid financial system in place also reduces stress and allows you to plan for both your personal and professional goals. By taking control of your finances, you're setting yourself up for a career that's not only fulfilling but financially secure, giving you the freedom to make choices that align with your life and legacy.

Tracking Income for Consistency and Growth

Tracking income isn't just about knowing how much you're making—it's about understanding patterns, predicting slow periods, and identifying opportunities to increase earnings. A consistent approach to income tracking helps you set realistic financial goals and ensures that you're always moving forward.

• Set Up a Simple Income Tracking System: Use a spreadsheet or financial app to record every payment, service, and client interaction. Include details like service type, frequency, and pricing to see which services bring in the most revenue.

• Review Monthly and Yearly Trends: Regularly review your income to spot patterns. Notice any peak times, slow seasons, or trends in client bookings, and use this information to plan promotions or special offerings during slower months.

• Create Income Goals: Based on your earnings, set monthly and yearly income goals. For example, if you want to increase earnings by 10% this year, break that down into monthly goals to keep you on track. Clear goals provide motivation and direction for consistent growth.

With an organized income tracking system, you're able to plan confidently, optimize high-earning services, and create a steady foundation for financial freedom.

Managing Expenses to Maximize Profit

Financial growth isn't just about earning more—it's about managing what you spend to maximize profit. Keeping a close eye on expenses ensures that your hard-earned income stays with you, supporting your financial goals and long-term stability.

• Categorize Essential and Non-Essential Expenses: Start by listing out your monthly and yearly expenses, dividing them into essentials (rent, supplies, utilities) and non-essentials (luxury items, extras). Knowing where your money is going allows you to make mindful adjustments that increase profitability.

•   Set a Budget for Supplies: Supplies are a significant cost for stylists, but a budget helps you stay in control. Compare suppliers, buy in bulk for savings, and keep an eye out for discounts. A budget ensures you have what you need without overspending.

•   Track Every Expense: Keep a record of every purchase related to your business, whether it's small tools, professional memberships, or marketing costs. Tracking these expenses gives you an accurate picture of your spending and highlights areas where you can cut back.

By managing expenses wisely, you're increasing profit without compromising quality, allowing more of your income to go toward your financial goals.

Client Retention as a Pillar of Financial Growth

A steady client base is essential for consistent income and financial growth. Client retention saves you from constantly seeking new clients, allowing you to focus on building strong relationships with those who return regularly, trust your expertise, and value your service.

•   Implement a Loyalty Program: Reward loyal clients with a simple loyalty program, offering a discount or bonus after a certain number of visits. This small incentive keeps clients coming back and shows appreciation for their continued support.

245

•   Personalize the Client Experience: Remembering details like a client's preferred style, favorite products, or upcoming events makes clients feel valued and encourages loyalty. These personal touches build a strong connection, increasing the likelihood of long-term retention.

•   Follow Up for Feedback: After a service, follow up with clients to ask about their satisfaction. A simple message thanking them for their visit and inviting feedback shows that you care about their experience, reinforcing trust and loyalty.

Retaining clients is more cost-effective than acquiring new ones, creating a reliable income stream that supports consistent financial growth.

Investing in Your Financial Future

Financial growth is about more than current earnings—it's about building a secure future. Smart investments, whether in your business, education, or retirement, create a foundation for long-term wealth and stability.

•   Set Aside a Portion for Reinvestment: Allocate a percentage of your income to reinvest in your business, whether it's for advanced training, new equipment, or marketing. Investing in your growth keeps your skills and brand competitive, ensuring ongoing client interest.

•   Create an Emergency Fund: Set up a savings account specifically for unexpected expenses. Aim for at least three months' worth of expenses saved, so you're prepared for slow periods or emergencies without financial stress.

•   Plan for Retirement: Begin setting aside funds for retirement, whether it's through a retirement account, investment portfolio, or savings plan. The earlier you start, the more you'll have to support your lifestyle and financial freedom in the future.

A proactive approach to investing in your financial future gives you peace of mind, ensuring that you're prepared for both opportunities and challenges as your career progresses.

Financial Growth Through Consistency and Smart Choices

Building a system for financial growth is about creating consistent income, managing expenses mindfully, and investing in your future. When you track your income, control your spending, and focus on client retention, you're building a career that's both profitable and stable. By taking a proactive approach to your finances, you're ensuring that each dollar works to support your goals and build the financial freedom you envision.

Financial freedom isn't just about reaching a certain number in your bank account—it's about creating a career where your hard work, skill, and dedication lead to a life that feels fulfilling, balanced, and secure. With a strong financial system in place, you're setting yourself up for long-term success, free from financial worries, and able to make choices that align with your vision for the future.

Planning for Longevity and Wealth Preservation

Why Longevity and Wealth Preservation Matter

Building wealth isn't just about making money—it's about creating financial security that lasts. As a stylist, you invest significant time and energy into your career, and planning for longevity ensures that your hard work translates into a stable, comfortable future. Wealth preservation is about maintaining what you earn, making wise financial decisions, and building a legacy that supports both your personal goals and professional aspirations.

When you focus on longevity, you're setting yourself up for a career that provides not only immediate rewards but also a future where you can enjoy financial freedom. This approach allows you to make choices that align with your long-term vision, supporting a life that's balanced, fulfilling, and secure.

Creating a Retirement Plan

A retirement plan is a key component of wealth preservation, providing the financial resources you need to enjoy life after years of dedication to your craft. Planning for retirement gives you the freedom to continue building your legacy, secure in the knowledge that you're financially prepared for the future.

- Set a Retirement Goal: Determine how much you want to have saved by the time you retire. Consider factors like your desired lifestyle, living expenses, and any travel or hobbies you plan to enjoy. This goal will guide your savings strategy and help you make informed decisions.

• Open a Retirement Account: Depending on your business setup, consider options like an IRA, Roth IRA, or a Solo 401(k). These accounts allow you to save and grow your money with tax advantages, making them effective tools for long-term savings.

• Contribute Consistently: Even small, regular contributions add up over time. Aim to set aside a percentage of your income each month specifically for retirement. Consistency is key; even if you start with modest amounts, regular contributions grow substantially over the years.

A retirement plan gives you peace of mind, knowing that each appointment and service is contributing to your financial future.

Investing to Grow and Preserve Wealth

Beyond retirement, investments can create additional streams of income, helping you grow wealth that supports both your current and future goals. Strategic investments also provide financial security, giving you the resources to weather any ups and downs in your career.

• Diversify Your Investments: Consider a mix of low-risk and moderate-risk investments to balance growth and security. Stocks, bonds, mutual funds, or real estate are all options to explore based on your comfort level and financial goals.

•   Invest in Your Business: Reinvesting in your business can yield significant returns. Whether it's advanced training, upgrading equipment, or expanding services, each investment in your career increases your earning potential, building a brand that's both reputable and profitable.

•   Stay Informed and Adjust as Needed: The investment landscape changes over time, so stay informed about market trends, interest rates, and investment options. Regularly review your portfolio and make adjustments to align with your goals, ensuring that your investments continue to support your wealth preservation strategy.

Investments create a financial cushion that protects your wealth, allowing you to plan with confidence and security.

Creating an Emergency Fund for Financial Stability

An emergency fund is essential for protecting your wealth and ensuring that you're prepared for unexpected expenses. Whether it's a slow season, a sudden personal expense, or an opportunity that requires quick action, an emergency fund provides the financial flexibility to handle it without stress.

•   Set a Savings Goal: Aim to save at least three to six months' worth of living and business expenses. This amount provides a reliable safety net, giving you the freedom to focus on your work without constantly worrying about financial setbacks.

•   Contribute Regularly: Treat your emergency fund as a non-negotiable expense, setting aside a portion of your income each month. Automating your savings can make this easier, ensuring that you're consistently building your safety net.

•   Use Only for True Emergencies: Discipline is key—avoid dipping into your emergency fund for non-essential expenses. By reserving this fund for genuine needs, you're ensuring that it's available when you need it most.

An emergency fund gives you stability and confidence, allowing you to approach your work with focus and peace of mind.

Managing Debt Wisely

Debt management is an essential part of wealth preservation. Minimizing and managing debt allows you to keep more of your income, ensuring that your hard-earned money is supporting your future goals instead of going toward interest payments.

•   Prioritize High-Interest Debt: Start by paying off high-interest debt first, such as credit card balances. Reducing high-interest debt saves you money over time, allowing you to redirect funds toward wealth-building efforts.

•   Consider Business Financing Carefully: If you're considering a loan or financing for business expansion, weigh the potential return against the cost. Only take on debt that's likely to bring in a return, and be mindful of the repayment terms.

•   Set a Debt Payoff Goal: Establish a realistic timeline for paying off your debt. Whether it's three, five, or ten years, having a goal keeps you motivated and focused, ensuring that debt doesn't limit your financial growth.

Wise debt management frees up more of your income for savings, investments, and the future you're building.

Passing on Your Legacy: Estate Planning

Estate planning isn't just about passing on wealth; it's about protecting what you've built and ensuring that your legacy supports the people and causes you care about. Estate planning allows you to designate how your assets will be managed, ensuring that your hard work continues to make a difference beyond your lifetime.

•   Create a Will or Trust: A will or trust ensures that your assets are distributed according to your wishes. If you have dependents or specific charities you want to support, an estate plan guarantees that they're taken care of.

        •   Choose Beneficiaries: Designate beneficiaries for any accounts, policies, or assets that allow it. This streamlines the process and ensures that your wealth goes directly to the people or causes you've chosen.

        •   Consult a Financial Planner: Estate planning can be complex, so consider consulting a financial planner or estate attorney. Their expertise ensures that your plan is comprehensive, legally sound, and aligned with your values.

An estate plan solidifies your legacy, ensuring that the wealth you've built serves a purpose that's meaningful to you.

Wealth Preservation as a Path to Financial Freedom

Longevity and wealth preservation are about creating a career where your financial growth endures, supporting you both today and in the future. By planning for retirement, investing strategically, and building a financial safety net, you're setting yourself up for stability, security, and the freedom to pursue your passions without financial limitations.

In the end, wealth preservation is about protecting what you've worked for, ensuring that each choice you make aligns with the vision you have for your life and legacy. With a commitment to longevity, careful planning, and disciplined choices, you're building a future where financial freedom isn't just a goal—it's a reality that supports a life of purpose, impact, and fulfillment.

Exercise: Creating Your Financial Freedom Plan

Step 1: Define Your Financial Freedom Goals

Start by identifying what financial freedom means to you. Think about both your immediate financial needs and your long-term goals, from lifestyle choices to future security.

- List Your Core Goals: Write down the goals that are most important to you, whether it's reaching a six-figure income, saving for retirement, or building a steady emergency fund. Each goal should reflect what financial freedom means specifically for you.

•   Set Timeframes for Each Goal: For each goal, assign a realistic timeframe. For example, you might aim to fully fund your emergency savings in one year or set aside a retirement amount over the next 10-15 years. Clear timelines provide structure and motivation for staying on track.

Defining your goals gives your financial plan direction, helping you prioritize and stay focused on the big picture.

Step 2: Create a Monthly Budget that Supports Your Goals

A budget is essential for turning financial goals into achievable milestones. Building a budget allows you to see exactly where your money is going, ensuring that each dollar is working to support your vision.

•   Divide Expenses into Categories: Start by listing out monthly expenses, such as rent, supplies, utilities, and savings contributions. Label each category as essential, business, or discretionary to prioritize spending.

•   Set a Savings Percentage: Decide on a percentage of your income to save each month. Aim for at least 10-20% of your income, if possible, to go directly toward savings, retirement, or investments.

•   Adjust as Needed: Keep your budget flexible. Review it monthly to ensure that it's still supporting your goals. Make adjustments when needed, allowing room for growth, increased savings, or new investment opportunities.

A budget aligned with your goals keeps you in control, allowing you to allocate resources with intention and purpose.

Step 3: Build a Consistent Savings and Investment Strategy

Financial freedom is built through consistent savings and smart investments. Developing a regular strategy for both ensures that your wealth grows over time, supporting your goals and future security.

- Automate Savings Contributions: Set up automatic transfers to savings or investment accounts. This consistency makes saving easier, allowing your wealth to grow with minimal effort.
- Choose an Investment Path: Whether it's mutual funds, stocks, real estate, or a retirement account, pick an investment that aligns with your comfort level and risk tolerance. Revisit your investment portfolio periodically to keep it aligned with your long-term goals.
- Plan for Retirement and Emergencies: Divide your savings between short-term security (emergency fund) and long-term goals (retirement). This dual focus gives you financial security both now and in the future.

A structured savings and investment plan lets your money work for you, building the financial foundation you need for true freedom.

Step 4: Track Progress and Make Adjustments

Your financial plan should grow with you. Regularly track your progress to see how you're moving toward your goals and make adjustments as needed.

- Review Monthly and Annually: At the end of each month, assess your progress toward savings and budget goals. Annually, take a big-picture look to adjust any long-term strategies.
- Celebrate Milestones: Recognize each financial milestone as it's achieved, whether it's a fully funded emergency account or meeting your income goal. Celebrating progress keeps you motivated and engaged with your plan.
- Adapt as Needed: Life and goals can change, so be open to adjusting your plan. Flexibility keeps your financial strategy resilient, allowing it to evolve as your career and vision grow.

Regular tracking reinforces your commitment to financial freedom, allowing you to see progress and adjust strategies to stay aligned with your goals.

Your Financial Freedom Plan: A Roadmap to Security and Success

With a personalized financial freedom plan, you're setting yourself up for a career that's profitable, stable, and focused on what matters most to you. This isn't just about income—it's about building a foundation that supports your lifestyle, vision, and future security. By consistently saving, budgeting with intention, and investing wisely, you're taking control of your financial destiny, creating a career and life defined by choice, freedom, and success.

Final Wrap-Up and Farewell

Summary of Key Takeaways

Congratulations on reaching the end of this journey! Throughout this book, you've explored the path from mastering your craft to building a profitable, impactful brand. You've learned the power of focused mastery, the importance of resilience, and the strategies for financial stability—all essential elements of a career that's both fulfilling and financially free.

By embracing specialization, you've set yourself apart as an expert, allowing you to attract clients who value your skill and commitment. Your focus on meaningful connections and community involvement has strengthened your brand, creating a legacy that goes beyond the chair. And with a clear financial plan, you're ensuring that each choice you make today supports the future you envision.

This journey is about more than success; it's about building a life and career that reflect who you are, what you value, and the impact you want to make. Each chapter, lesson, and strategy has prepared you to achieve not only your financial goals but also a legacy that uplifts and inspires others.

Farewell Message

As you move forward, remember that every step of this journey is an opportunity to grow, refine, and build something meaningful. You've laid the foundation for a career that combines purpose with prosperity, proving that it's possible to create lasting impact while achieving financial freedom. Keep your vision clear, your goals focused, and your commitment strong.

Your journey is yours to shape—continue to master your craft, inspire your clients, and build a brand that's truly unforgettable. Here's to the impact you're creating, the wealth you're building, and the legacy you're leaving. Keep going, and never stop striving for excellence.

Influential Works

The following resources have shaped my understanding of mastery, client relationships, and financial growth. While not directly cited, these works have contributed to the principles and insights shared in Pixie to Profit. I hope these resources inspire you as they have inspired me, offering further exploration into the art of focused mastery and building a meaningful, financially rewarding career.

1.   **The E-Myth Revisited by Michael Gerber**
Gerber's insights on creating systems and structuring a business for success are invaluable for any professional looking to move from solo work to building a sustainable, efficient enterprise.

2. Deep Work by Cal Newport

Newport's exploration of focused work and mastery highlights the power of narrowing one's focus, a principle that reinforces the benefits of specializing in a niche.

3. Rich Dad Poor Dad by Robert Kiyosaki

This book offers a foundational perspective on financial independence and the mindset needed to build wealth, focusing on making money work for you through smart financial habits.

4. Your Money or Your Life by Vicki Robin

Robin's work on financial growth and intentional living emphasizes the value of aligning finances with life goals, a perspective that can transform both personal and professional financial planning.

5. Influence: The Psychology of Persuasion by Robert Cialdini

Cialdini's exploration of psychology and persuasion offers valuable insights into client relationships, loyalty, and building trust, reinforcing the importance of understanding client psychology in the beauty industry.

6. African American (Black Women) Beauty and Style Icons

Various articles and books on the contributions of Black women to beauty and fashion history have been influential in appreciating the pixie cut's evolution. Icons like Halle Berry and Josephine Baker, among others, have shaped the cultural significance of short haircuts, highlighting their strength, elegance, and resilience.

ACKNOWLEDGEMENTS

First, I recognize my Creator, whose grace and guidance have led me through every step of this journey. With faith as my foundation, I find strength, resilience, and clarity in my purpose.

I give honor to my mother, who has given me jewels not only in my career but first in my life. Her wisdom and strength have been the foundation I've built upon, guiding me with love and purpose in all I do.

To my children, who have been patient with me, who help me grow, and who bring new meaning to my life—you are my inspiration and motivation. Each of you adds to my purpose, reminding me of the legacy I'm building.

And to the one and only love of my life, whose presence is both my anchor and my light. You have imparted so much of yourself into me, shaping my spirit and strengthening my heart. Your unwavering support, kindness, and wisdom remind me every day of what it means to love fully and be truly seen. With you, I find fulfillment in the journey, knowing that no matter the path, we walk it together. I am profoundly grateful to share this world with you, at this time, in this life, where your love enriches every moment.

INDEX

E

F

G

H

I

About the Author

Miko Pierson McAlmon is a celebrated stylist, educator, and entrepreneur, with over 30 years of hands-on experience in the beauty industry. As the founder of Miko HairCare Systems and Miko Pierson Cosmo Education, Miko has built a legacy centered on excellence, empowerment, and innovation in haircare. Known for her mastery of short cuts and textured styling, she has dedicated her career to helping clients feel confident and stylists find their unique path to success. Recognized as the go-to expert in her community for pixie cuts and client-focused experiences, Miko has earned the loyalty and trust of a dedicated clientele.

Beyond the salon, Miko is a passionate educator committed to guiding other stylists toward fulfilling, profitable careers. Through her teaching programs, she empowers beauty professionals to embrace focused mastery, build meaningful client relationships, and achieve financial freedom. Her work is grounded in the belief that every stylist has the potential to create a brand that reflects their passion and expertise.

In Pixie to Profit, Miko shares her proven strategies and insights, drawn from decades of industry experience, to help stylists everywhere elevate their craft, build loyal client bases, and create a lasting impact in the industry.

Stay Connected

Let's keep in touch! Follow me for more tips, resources, and inspiration on social media, or reach out through my website and email:

- Website: www.mikopierson.com
- Instagram: @MikoPierson
- Facebook: MikoPierson
- Email: info@mikopierson.com

Thank you for joining me on this journey. I can't wait to hear about yours!

ABOUT THE PUBLISHER

Pixie to Profit is published by Swiner Publishing, a company dedicated to supporting authors from all backgrounds and industries. Swiner Publishing offers comprehensive guidance and resources to help individuals bring their work to life, whether they're publishing for the beauty industry, business, personal development, or beyond.

Made in the USA
Columbia, SC
21 February 2025

54177757R20146